The Relaxation Letters

Printed on Recycled Paper

The Relaxation Letters

*Insights from the Famous on Life,
Love and Well-Being*

Audrey Burns Ross

Aquarian/Thorsons
An Imprint of HarperCollins*Publishers*

The Aquarian Press
An Imprint of HarperCollins*Publishers*
77–85 Fulham Palace Road,
Hammersmith, London W6 8JB

Published by The Aquarian Press 1993
1 3 5 7 9 10 8 6 4 2

Audrey Burns Ross asserts the moral right to
be identified as the author of this work

A catalogue record for this book
is available from the British Library

ISBN 1 85538 371 3

Illustrations by Josephine Sumner

Phototypeset by Harper Phototypesetters Limited,
Northampton, England
Printed in Great Britain by
HarperCollinsManufacturing Glasgow

For Edwin and Gayle, who have believed in this project as much as I – with all my love.

A PRAYER

You're winning.
You simply cannot fail.
The only obstacle is doubt.

I should also like to dedicate this book to the memory of my dear friend Jane Longmore. It was she who encouraged me to realize an idea that had been in my mind for many years. One day in the Autumn of 1990 I visited her at Guy's Hospital in London. We were talking about our lives and I shared with her my idea to compile *The Relaxation Letters;* she gave me the inspiration to begin the book.

By the time she died in May 1991 I had just seven contributions. Almost her last words to me were: 'If you can get seven, you can get a hundred and seven.'

~~~~~~

Acknowledgments

This book exists because of the deep commitment to it by many people worldwide. I have been deeply touched that so many people have taken the time to share their personal reflections on life and *The Relaxation Letters* are testament to their insight, wisdom, humour and love of life. My sincere thanks go to all my contributors.

My gratitude is indeed profound to Geraldine Deaver, one of the contributors. For the first eighteen months all my work was done in longhand. Then, in the Spring of 1992, Geraldine joined me to do the typing and has been with me on a voluntary basis to the end of the work. I shall always remember my rushed trips by train to Peterborough, our lingering Sunday lunches, her wise counsel, absolute commitment to the book and our friendship which has evolved during this period.

I am also indebted to my mother for helping me with research and to all those, too numerous to mention, who have encouraged and supported me throughout; I am also grateful for the many introductions I have had.

My grateful thanks also go to Elizabeth Puttick and Rosemary Staheyeff at Thorsons/Aquarian Publishers. Their understanding, encouragement and guidance were much appreciated by this raw recruit to the world of publishing.

I thank them all for understanding what I have been trying to do and why!

~~~~~~

Contents

Preface   viii

List of Contributors   xi

THE LETTERS   1

Permission Acknowledgments   177

Preface

Modern life can sometimes appear overwhelming. Amidst the stresses and strains, how can we find peace of mind and retain a positive outlook?

The change in my own life came about twenty-six years ago. Following the example of an aunt, I attended one of the earliest Yoga classes held in Edinburgh. It is difficult to put into words what happened to me that day but I seemed to become aware of a part of myself which hitherto I had not known existed, and, left the class that night with such a wonderful feeling of heightened awareness, stillness and relaxation. The stress had somehow disappeared and for the first time I felt I could really see my way. The wonderful thing was that this had come about through very natural, simple methods and did not cost a lot of money.

Prompted by an inner urge which I could not ignore, I resolved then that a part of my life would be spent sharing this knowledge with as many people as possible.

Many years have passed since then and many things have changed in my life. This resolve has remained undiminished, however.

I was also aware as time went by that many of the simple things in life which we take for granted were in fact sources of tremendous peace of mind and relaxation. Although my own particular way was guided by Yogic philosophy, I realized there were other paths one could follow to gain this spiritual enrichment. For that reason, it occurred to me that a compilation of the philosophy and relaxation techniques of a variety of people from many walks of life throughout the world might be an uplifting source of encouragement to others, as well as being generally interesting. I decided that this should also include any words which had given them inspiration during their lives. As Hazrat Inayat Khan said: 'The words that enlighten the soul are more precious than jewels.'

I therefore posed the following three questions to my contributors:

How do you relax and unwind?
What is your general philosophy of life?
Do you have a poem, passage or any words that have given you inspiration in your lifetime?

In view of the very personal nature of the questions, I told the contributors not to answer all of them unless they wished. You will see from the answers how differently they have tackled them and this, I believe, is this book's great strength.

I had no way of knowing when I began this work that midway through its compilation the way of life I had known up to that point would be brought to a dramatic end and that I would be faced with what was to become the most difficult period of my life. Of course, the inner spiritual strength accumulated over many years of Yoga practice played a big part in coping with the crisis, and, I always knew that if I could treat the highs and lows of my life with equal equanimity I would always be a survivor. However, I can truly say that we as a family have been constantly uplifted and helped by the content of letters arriving from contributors. I know from firsthand experience, therefore, the strength of this book, which may be instrumental as a guiding force in your life. I hope you will use it time and time again, and that it may serve as the beginning of a very exciting journey. Life CAN be an exciting journey. I hope this book enriches yours.

When I decided that all the proceeds of this book should go to charitable causes, there was no question in my mind as to which charities I would choose to support: The Friends of the Earth, whose efforts to safeguard our fragile and beautiful planet are an inspiration to us all, and UNICEF,

which displays an untiring commitment to helping the poor, unwanted
and unhappy children of the world. I shall be closely involved in the
decision as to how and where to allocate the money in each case.

Audrey Brms Ross.

List of Contributors

Sir Hardy Amies, KCVO, RDI, FRSA
Walter H. Annenberg, KBE (Hon)
The Lady Elizabeth Anson
Dr Mary Archer
Lord Archer of Weston-Super-Mare
The Rt. Hon. Paddy Ashdown, MP
Dame Josephine Barnes, DBE, FRCP, FRCS, FRCOG
Mauro D. Beltrandi
The Rt. Hon. Tony Benn, MP
Sir Isaiah Berlin, OM, CBE
Hon. Benazir Bhutto
Colonel John Blashford-Snell, MBE
Rabbi Lionel Blue
Chris Bonington, CBE
P. W. Botha, DMS
Molly Bown
Patrick Burns
The Most Reverend and Right Hon. George Carey, The Archbishop of Canterbury
Ian Carmichael
Dame Barbara Cartland, DBE, D.St.J.
The Rt. Hon. Helen Clark, PC, MP
Dame Catherine Cookson, DBE, OBE
Henry Cooper, OBE, KSG
Joseph Corvo
Constance Cummings, CBE
The Dalai Lama XIV
Pierre Daninos
Geraldine Deaver
Dame Judi Dench, DBE, OBE
The late Monica Dickens, MBE
The Lady Dulverton
Anne Dunhill
Her Serene Highness Princess Elizabeth de Croÿ

Bridge Ennis
Sir Ranulph Fiennes, OBE
Shreela, The Baroness Flather
Bryan Forbes
The Very Revd Graham Forbes
Anna Ford
Christina Foyle
Clare Francis, MBE
Dame Phyllis Frost, AC, DBE, CBE
David Gee
Bob Geldof, KBE
Peter Gellhorn, FGSM
Susan George
Sir Alexander Gibson, Kt., CBE
Sir John Gielgud, CH
Graham Gooch, OBE
Carolyn Grace
Billy Graham
Dr Vartan Gregorian
The Rt. Hon. The Lord Hanson
Sir John Harvey-Jones, MBE
Sir Michael Hordern, CBE
Bishop Trevor Huddleston, CR
Sir Peter Imbert, QPM
Jeremy Irons
Glenda Jackson, MP
Cornelis de Jager
Derek Jameson
Surgeon Commander Rick Jolly, OBE, Royal Navy
Deborah Kerr
Glenys Kinnock
The Rt. Hon. Neil Kinnock, MP
Helmut Kohl
Wim Kok
The Rt. Hon. Ian Lang, MP

Jane Lapotaire
Julian Lloyd Webber
The Rt. Hon. The Earl of Longford, KG, PC
Dr Tom Burns McArthur
Feri McArthur
Hamish MacInnes, OBE, BEM
Virginia McKenna
Clare Maxwell-Hudson
Dame Jean Maxwell-Scott, DCVO
June Mendoza, RP, ROI
Michael Meyer
Keith Michell
Bishop Hugh Montefiore
Roger Moore
Frederick Muller
Dr Anna Maria Neuhold
Conor Cruise O'Brien
Edna O'Brien
Iona Opie
The Rt. Hon. The Lord Owen of the City of Plymouth
Sir Peter Parker, LVO
The Rt. Hon. The Lord Parry of Neyland, Dyfed
Nicholas Parsons
Jonathon Porritt
Marguerite Porter
Dame Shirley Porter, DBE, DL
Syed A. Rafique
Kathleen Raine, D.Litt., D.Litt., D.Litt.
Irina Ratushinskaya
Claire Rayner
Beryl Reid, OBE
Trewin Restorick
Dr Jonathan Rhoads, MD
Angela Rippon
Anita Roddick, OBE

The Rt. Hon. Dame Angela Rumbold, DBE, CBE, MP
Anthony Russell-Roberts
Lady Ryder of Warsaw, CMG, OBE
Dr Steven B. Sample
Charles Secrett
Dennis Selinger
Peter Shilton, MBE
Antoinette Sibley, CBE
Robert Smith
Sir Georg Solti, KBE
Tommy Steele, OBE
Jackie Stewart, OBE
Dr Elisabeth D. Svendsen, MBE, DVMS
Mother Teresa, MC, Hon. OM, Hon. OBE
Richard Todd, OBE
Chaim Topol
Bill Travers
Dorothy Tutin, CBE
The Most Reverend Desmond M. Tutu, DD, FKC
Dame Ninette de Valois, CH, DBE, CBE
Rev. Dr Chad Varah, OBE
Joni Van Der Veen
The Rt. Hon. The Lord Weatherill
Simon Weston, OBE
Fatima Whitbread, MBE
Mary Whitehouse, CBE
The Rt. Hon. The Lord Wilson of Rievaulx, KG, OBE, FRS
Lady Wilson of Rievaulx
Michael Winner
Fay Woolf
The Marchioness of Worcester
Susannah York
Dr Sir Gideon A. P. Zoleveke, KBE, MBE

Sir Hardy Amies, KCVO, RDI, FRSA

Dressmaker by Appointment to H.M. The Queen since 1955;
Director, Hardy Amies Ltd. since 1946

I try not to get into a state from which I have to unwind and succeed
– mostly.

I do a lot of needlepoint – seriously – *never* from what is called a
'kit', always from carefully planned designs which are either put onto
canvas or made into a chart, all by the Royal School of Needlework.

This requires attention and I don't think I would start to work if I
were in a state.

I have not yet found any clue to explain why I am on this earth.
However, I can look back over nearly a century (born 1909) and I think
I am very lucky to have lived now. There are so many things to enjoy
– wonderful air travel: Concorde to New York. I think back to the horrors
of 1945: Shannon and Newfoundland for New York.

I go to Australia in October. It will be at least my tenth trip and it
holds no fears for me. I shall stop in New York where we – the firm
– have had a flat for 20 years.

In three years time I shall celebrate – WE shall celebrate – the 50th
anniversary of Maison Amies. H.M. The Queen has generously made
me a Knight, just for doing my duty.

I am sure we are meant to enjoy life. You cannot do this if you cheat
or are unkind. However, you must be determined to fulfil yourself. In
fighting to do this, one must try and not hurt people but *your* life is the
most important thing you have to nurture.

Walter H. Annenberg, KBE (HON)

United States Ambassador to the Court of St James's, 1969–74

In response to your seeking 'How you relax and unwind' I have something of a problem.

Although I am now 84 years of age, I am as busy as I ever was, largely in philanthropic affairs, and quite frankly, find it difficult to relax and unwind.

Philosophically, I believe that it is important for young people to experience some adversity because if a young person has a measure of good character, adversity will inspire to overcome; and without good character, a young person probably won't amount to much.

Again, philosophically, while I am grateful for a challenging and exciting life, it seems that in the scheme of things, harassment is just around the corner, and we have to be on guard as it is necessary to be able to handle it successfully.

I have another item that preys on my mind from time to time because it was an utterance of one of the world's great philosophers, Immanuel Kant (1724–1804): 'Out of the crooked timber of humanity, no straight line was ever made.' (This was translated into English from German and is an acceptable translation by recognized scholars.) I must admit that I have seen honorable and able human beings suddenly do something that is unacceptable, and while this is perplexing, I do think of the words of Immanuel Kant.

Walter Annenberg

The Lady Elizabeth Anson

Party Planners Proprietress

I relax and unwind in many different ways. Pulling out bindweed in the garden is very therapeutic, as is stringing beans and shelling peas. Croquet, jigsaws and crosswords provide more passive ways to unwind, and a favourite pastime is making ice-cream from different berries that I have picked.

My philosophy of life is to treat people in the way that I would like to be treated and to give as much pleasure to others in life as they have given to me.

The following words have inspired me throughout my life, and give me comfort and courage when it is needed:

> God grant me the serenity to accept the things
> I cannot change, courage to change the things I
> can and wisdom to know the difference.
>
> REINHOLD NIEBUHR

Dr Mary Archer

Scientist

I am hardly an authority on relaxation techniques, unless relaxation may be obtained by change of occupation. I enjoy singing, and am choirmistress of the local church choir, and I also find squash relaxing in a strenuous sort of way! If I have a general philosophy of life, I suppose it is not to bite off more than I can chew, but to chew what I do bite off.

Lord Archer of Weston-Super-Mare

The former Jeffrey Archer, Politician and Author

I am sorry to tell you that I am quite incapable of relaxing, although I do enjoy a game of squash in the morning and watching Somerset play cricket. Other than that work is what I enjoy most.

My favourite quote is from Longfellow:

The heights by great men reached and kept
　Were not attained by sudden flight,
But they, while their companions slept,
　Were toiling upward in the night.

> HENRY WADSWORTH LONGFELLOW
> (1807–82), 'THE LADDER OF SAINT
> AUGUSTINE'

The Rt. Hon. Paddy Ashdown, MP

Leader of the Social and Liberal Democrats since 1988

Perhaps you would like to consider the following, which comes from *The Gulag Archipelago* by Solzhenitsyn:

> Live with a steady superiority over life – don't be afraid of misfortune and do not yearn after happiness; it is, after all, the same: the bitter doesn't last forever and the sweet never fills the cup to overflowing. It is enough if you don't freeze in the cold and if thirst and hunger don't claw at your insides.

Dame Josephine Barnes, DBE, FRCP, FRCS, FRCOG

President of the British Medical Association 1979–80;
the first ever woman president

I relax and unwind by walking. As I live near Holland Park I find that at any time of the day, whatever the weather, if I walk around the park, which takes about forty minutes, I become completely relaxed. Otherwise, when I am in the country I walk whenever possible and I enjoy walking around London.

My general philosophy of life has been to spend what time I have in the way that is most profitable and useful, in particular to other people. It has been my privilege as a gynaecologist to serve many thousands of women and their babies and I regard myself as fortunate in having had the opportunity to do this.

Mauro D. Beltrandi

Italian Petroleum Geologist

My life, my profession and my interests have always been inspired by nature. It is only in 'nature' that I have ever found my moments of real detachment; of total physical and spiritual freedom.

How do I 'switch-off' and relax? By reverting to moments in my life when I was totally absorbed in, and captivated by 'nature'.

The sunset in the desert; the colours, the peace and the silence.

The immensity of the Sahara; the indescribable panorama from a high cliff, above the edge of the great sand-sea, overlooking the distant dry valleys and lakes, where life once flowed and flowered in the 'cradle of mankind'.

The majesty of the Arctic; the delicate colours of the sea and the sky in a morning in Greenland.

The Alps with their glaciers and snow-capped mountains and the splendour of the misty valleys below.

The peace, delicacy and tenderness of a woodland in Scotland on an autumn morning.

The ecstasy of making love on the warm sand, near the sea, with the fragrance of dry sea-weed wafting in a gentle breeze.

The vision of the sea from the windows and terrace of my house on the Island of Elba.

And so many, many more moments in nature. It is in these memories that I find my relaxation.

As you are probably aware, I am a geologist by profession – but I am also a geologist by instinct. In fact, I am convinced that I was born a geologist. I grew up on the Northern Italian coast, on a narrow strip of land between high mountains and sea. In my youth I ran by the sea and climbed the mountains that were so close and easy to reach – and at that time, so unspoiled and preserved. Even as a young boy I had an almost insatiable desire to understand the mystery of the beauty by which I was surrounded.

Perhaps, because my profession required that I deal daily with the history of the world, over millions of years, I was provided a certain protection, or even refuge, from everyday life and its related problems. I am able to perceive the dramatic exiguity of our presence on earth, compared to the immensity of the universe and the story of the world and its continuous evolution.

Consequently, when I need or want to 'switch-off' from the trials and tribulations of daily life, in which 'volente or dolente' I am involved, I relive the special moments of my life when I was absorbed in my passionate love of 'nature'. To capture again these moments in time is rather like capturing a small piece of this immensity, in which one is included, and which one too often tends to neglect. I find my relaxation in its secret existence and continuous progression.

M.D. Peetrand.

The Rt. Hon. Tony Benn, MP

Former Labour Cabinet Minister; Author

I enjoy my work which is my main interest.

I relax with my family – four children and seven grandchildren.

A mug of tea and a pipe are a comfort at all times.

My favourite quotation is from the American theologian Reinhold Niebuhr (a family friend) who wrote:

Man's capacity for evil makes Democracy necessary.
Man's capacity for good makes Democracy possible.

Sir Isaiah Berlin, OM, CBE

Fellow of All Souls College, Oxford;
President of the British Academy 1974–78

I wish I could answer your letter. I have no idea when and how I relax, if I do; nor do I have a general philosophy of life. So what can I say?

Hon. Benazir Bhutto

Former Prime Minister of Pakistan; Leader Pakistan People's Party

I do not practise Yoga now because it is difficult to find the time. However, when I was in solitary confinement during the years of dictatorship I taught myself Yoga. It helped me cope with stress, with loneliness and also helped me stay healthy. People who practise Yoga or meditation have a lovely glow on their faces which comes from their facial muscles being relaxed rather than pinched with tension. I can always recognize one from a distance. Yoga also helps powers of concentration and develops a positive mental approach. The world is within us, as is peace, if only we paused enough to look inside.

Benazir Bhutto.

Colonel John Blashford-Snell, MBE

On the staff of the Ministry of Defence since 1983;
Leader of different expeditions to remote parts of the world

For inspiration I turn to the following:

'There's no sense in going further – it's the edge of cultivation,'
So they said, and I believed it – broke my land and sowed
my crop –

Built my barns and strung my fences in the little border
station
Tucked away below the foothills where the trails run out
and stop.

Till a voice, as bad as Conscience, rang interminable changes
On one everlasting Whisper day and night repeated – so:
'Something hidden. Go and find it. Go and look behind
the Ranges –
'Something lost behind the Ranges. Lost and waiting
for you. Go!'

RUDYARD KIPLING (1865–1936), 'THE EXPLORER', 1898

Rabbi Lionel Blue

*Lecturer, Leo Baeck College, London since 1967; Convener of the
Beth Din (Ecclesiastical Court) of the Reform Synagogues of
Great Britain 1971–88; Broadcaster and Writer*

I relax by browsing around charity shops; contemplating in silent
synagogues and monasteries; reading books with happy endings.

My philosophy of life: To get to my true home which is Heaven.

I have been inspired by a chance remark regarding life which I
overheard: 'Don't take it too heavy dear, don't take it too heavy.'

Chris Bonington, CBE

Mountaineer, Writer and Photographer

When I am at home and working on a book or planning an expedition I usually spend the morning in my office and often as a way of relaxing and unwinding at lunchtime I go running over the fells, which are at the back of our house. I take our dogs Bella and Bodie with me. Sometimes, my wife Wendy and I just go for a long walk over the fells. They are always beautiful whatever the weather and being out on them is the best way I know of leaving work behind for a time.

P. W. Botha, DMS

State President Republic of South Africa 1984–89;
Prime Minister and Minister of National Intelligence Service 1978–84

I wish to inform you that after my retirement I keep myself busy with daily strolls along the sea, overlooking activities on my small holding not far from my home.

Relaxation is receiving friends and other interested people, and co-operating with the Institute for Contemporary History at one of our universities where we donated most of my private documents, which are being used for writing a biography. Furthermore we are interested in local organizations such as the Tourist Association, local Ratepayers Association and the local Museum; and from time to time we visit our children and they visit us. So every day has enough of its own good as far as we are concerned.

You wish me to send you a quote. I would say: 'Do your duty and continue building your hope in the merciful God and Jesus Christ. The great secret of life is the happiness you achieve when you provide love to others and receive love from those who take a real interest in you.'

Molly Bown

The Head of The Francis Holland Junior School, London

My bath is the one place where no one can disturb me – bliss! I should like to add that a glass of champagne in one hand and a good book in the other can also alleviate the stresses and strains of daily life!! Unfortunately, these additions are not a daily occurrence.

My philosophy of life: friendship – to be a good friend and to have good friends is the fruit of life.

I am inspired by the following words:

A Friend
A friend is a person who is for you always . . .
He wants nothing from you except that you be yourself.
He is the one being with whom you can feel safe. With him
you can utter your heart, its badness and its goodness.
Like the shade of a great tree in the noonday heat is a friend.
Like the home port with your country's flag flying after a long
journey is a friend. A friend is an impregnable citadel of
refuge in the strife of existence. It is he that keeps alive
your faith in human nature, that makes you believe that it is
a good universe. He is the antidote to despair, the elixir of
hope, the tonic for depression – Give to him without reluctance.

ANON

Molly Bown.

~~~~~~

Patrick Burns

BBC Political Editor (Midlands)

RELAXATION

From the top floor at Pebble Mill, the sharp-eyed among us can make out the score on the board at Edgbaston cricket ground. In between stands my home. This is how I balance work and play.

The 'play' part is simple enough. I am a member of Warwickshire Cricket Club: the gasps of a Test Match crowd can be heard from my beloved garden. Living within a short walk of the ground is one of my great self-indulgences: 'dog day' afternoons then a stroll home, while the rest of the crowd are barely halfway back to their cars.

Paradoxically, it is the 'work' side of the equation that gives me scope for relaxation. My brisk walk to Pebble Mill is more than just a sop to my post-athletic conscience; it also avoids one of the most stressful timewasters of this modern age: commuting. I am fortunate that the BBC chose to locate its Birmingham HQ in a changeless little corner of inner suburbia surrounded by parks, a nature centre, golf courses and more acres of trees than the Bois de Boulogne.

And then there is music; for me perhaps the greatest therapy of all. When not even the classiest CD will quite do the trick, we have a ten-minute drive to Symphony Hall, which Simon Rattle famously has pioneered as his artistic home. I am unable to hear anything by Beethoven or Mozart without feeling a shiver of excitement.

Finally, home again as Voltaire would have it 'to cultivate my own garden'. Tending my roses, giving them new life, revitalizes me. The numb mindless free-wheeling of mowing the lawn is the natural antidote to professional hyper-activity. And when the grass is close-cropped, I swing some gentle overs for my eight-year-old son to drive to all corners.

~~~~~~

Someday perhaps 'J. P. Burns' will be named on that famous scoreboard.

PHILOSOPHY OF LIFE

Some years ago – more than I care to remember – I found myself preparing for an especially important programme interview. Should I shrink from asking the obvious question simply because it was obvious? No! The 'obvious question' is precisely what the viewer usually wants to see and hear answered. So, with Sir David Attenborough duly installed in front of me, out with thudding predictability came my opening gambit: 'Sir David, to what do you attribute your fascination with animals?'

My banal overture was accorded a disproportionately high reward. An answer that has stayed with me ever since. 'Only an adult', he announced, 'could ask that question. To any child, a fascination with animals is an accepted part of life. Unfortunately *some* people lose it when they turn into grown-ups.'

My own philosophy stems from the notion that we should preserve somewhere within ourselves a place for our childhood to linger on a while. Keeping alive the elements of surprise, wonder, curiosity and sheer excitement that fire high-octane young imaginations.

Naive? Perhaps. But consider the 'adult' alternative. The cynical semi-detached 'cool' that flattens out the intriguing nuances, the romance, and yes the sheer joy of being alive. So often we hear 'adults' considering how marvellous it must be to see the world through the eyes of a child. I urge them to try! They have nothing to lose but their conceit: the tired 'seen it all before, older and wiser' mentality.

Of course we have to deal with the harsh realities of life. But to be able still to rejoice in the elegant, fragrant unfurling of a rosebud is to preserve the inner Humanity and the Youth, that in the end can make sense of it all.

Now that I have two children, I see the learning process is a two-way affair. They may have much to learn from us, but we have no less to gain from them. Each day I spend with James and Helen I undergo instruction: how wonderful that the duck is so beautifully designed for swimming! How clever that the bee helps pollenate the flowers in its single-minded quest for nectar.

Are these obvious answers to yet more 'obvious questions'? I think not.

Ask Sir David.

The Most Reverend and Right Hon. George Carey, The Archbishop of Canterbury

I've chosen Herbert's evocative lines because they outline the complex shape of prayer. Prayer for me is far more than words – it is a relationship with God who is a Friend, Lord and Father. The last two words say it all – 'something understood'.

Prayer the Church's banquet. Angel's age.
God's breath in man returning to his birth.
The soul in paradise, heart in pilgrimage.
The Christian plummet sounding heav'n and earth:

Engine against th' Almighty, sinners' tower.
Reversed thunder. Christ-side-piercing spear.
The six days world transposing in an hour.
A kind of tune, which all things hear and fear:

Softness and peace and joy, and love, and bliss.
Exalted Manna, gladness of the best.
Heaven in ordinary, man well drest.
The milky way, the bird of paradise.

Church-bells beyond the stars heard, the soul's blood.
The land of spices: something understood.

GEORGE HERBERT (1593–1633)

✝ George Cantuar

Author's note: *Cantuariensis* is the Latin for the adjective meaning 'belonging to Canterbury', abbreviated normally to Cantuar. It is traditional for the Archbishop of Canterbury to use this as his signature. The cross signifies a bishop.

21

Ian Carmichael

Actor

I'm afraid your writing to me on this subject is rather laughable as I am notorious amongst my associates for having no power of relaxation whatsoever!

The philosophy of life that I try to follow (not always successfully) is one espoused by the essayist Logan Pearsall Smith:

There are two things to aim at in life:
first, to get what you want; and after that,
to enjoy it. Only the wisest of mankind achieve
the second.

Dame Barbara Cartland, DBE, D.St.J.

Authoress and Playwright

I do not deliberately relax except when I go to sleep.

I take honey when I go to bed, and would never think of taking the Doctors' medicines of any sort.

No one has died of not sleeping yet, and if I am awake at night I tell myself a story or listen to music.

I am the Founder and President of the National Association for Health and I take a lot of vitamins, as I try all those which come on to the market. If they are successful I recommend them to the 30,000 people who write to me every year about health.

My philosophy of life is summed up in the enclosed poem, which I wrote.

A Prayer

One thing I know, life can never die,
  Translucent, splendid, flaming like the sun.
Only our bodies wither and deny
  The life force when our strength is done.

Let me transmit this wonderful fire,
  Even a little through my heart and mind,
Bringing the perfect love we all desire
  To those who seek, yet blindly cannot find.

We each give to the world as much of the Life Force as can flow uninhibited through our confining bodies. This is our task, the reason we exist to transmit the godhead through us. How poorly we succeed, and how much more successful we could be!

BARBARA CARTLAND

Rt. Hon. Helen Clark, PC, MP

New Zealand Deputy Leader of the Opposition

As member of Parliament for Mt Albert, Labour Spokesperson on Health and Labour, and Deputy Leader of the Opposition, I seize the few opportunities I get to relax and unwind. I love travelling and do so whenever I can. I also enjoy reading, going to the theatre and films, and occasionally indulge in some Asian cooking.

Helen Clark.

Dame Catherine Cookson, DBE, OBE

Author, since 1950

PHILOSOPHY

If I hadn't been brought up in an atmosphere of want, drink, and ceaseless hard work, threaded with faint veins of love and unexpected and less-understood spurts of joy, I should now not be known as Catherine Cookson the writer, because this environment was the womb in which my imagination was bred.

That I refused to accept this fact until the umbilical cord was severed by a breakdown I now look upon as part of the plan that was designed at my conception when my mother committed the unforgivable sin of giving herself in love to a man without words having first been spoken over them by a parson, a priest, or a registrar.

The kitchen of 10, William Black Street, East Jarrow, in the County of Durham was a world of its own. It was ruled over by my step-grandfather, John McMullen, a drunken, ignorant Irishman, who could neither read nor write; a man who worked hard, said little and was lost on the empty plane of his silence and ignorance but who nevertheless was the only man in my young life, and the one who has left the most lasting impression.

It was this old man who first told me I had two of the main ingredients that go to make a writer, a vivid imagination and, as he said, sprouting from that I was a natural liar.

John McMullen was feared by most people; somehow I was never afraid of him. As he once said to me, he had never wished me to be born, but then he had made the best of a bad job, and we had shaken hands on it.

It was evident all my young days that he was the man in my life. This was made clear every night when he came in at tea-time and sat down to a meal of either finny haddie and new bread, or steak and chips, or panhackelty. But always he would start the meal with an egg, and I had to have the top of it; the top meant the egg being cut in half, and he would scoop the contents on to a piece of dripping and bread and hand it to me, and I would stand by his side and eat it.

I often wondered over the years why I couldn't have an egg to myself, but no, as I said, he was the man in my life, he was the man who was bringing me up, feeding me, and this had to be made evident. Of course, no credit was given to my mother who worked sixteen hours a day, often eight hours outside the house and eight hours in, looking after him and my ailing grandmother and a half-brother and numerous lodgers. No credit was ever given to her, she was just Our Kate, and she had sinned grievously; she should thank her lucky stars that she had a roof over her head and she wasn't in the workhouse, and me along of her.

In those days at the beginning of the century there were many such people as Kate and myself but who were less fortunate and who'd had to find refuge in the workhouse, and there the mother was forced to remain until the child was fourteen and could itself go out to work.

Years later when I went to work in South Shields Workhouse I shuddered inwardly as I looked at some of the inmates and thought: There but for the grace of God goes Our Kate. And when I had to take mothers to the cottage homes I would repeat the saying as I looked at the children: There, but for the grace of God, goes me.

But all the while I was gaining something, a philosophy you could say. I was learning that philosophy isn't the prerogative of the academic, the intellectual, all those supposedly knowledgeable people who blind you with the science of the mind. Philosophy is, as I saw it then and still do, the essence of the thinking of every ordinary man and woman. It is the sum total of what they have drained out of their living whether through sorrow or joy, satisfaction or frustration.

I have come to my own particular philosophy by being educated in a hard school where lessons of poverty, shame, inferiority, fear and ill-health were hard to learn. But my philosophy evolved, as I see it now, in my fight against these afflictions. I was helped, I suppose, in its fostering by my vivid imagination, my sensitivity and my groping to understand my fellow creatures, those nearest to me.

But, even so, it was slow to evolve and, of course, I wasn't conscious that I was learning the lessons of life when I attacked my afflictions with aggressiveness and ambition. It wasn't really until I learned to apply the salve of compassion to the wounds of my own life that I realized I had garnered one grain of wisdom.

I could wish I had become wise to do so many things much earlier, but then it is in the blissfulness of ignorance that so much is learned and achieved, and this, I suppose, is the basic purpose of life.

Whenever I speak of me granda or Our Kate it recalls the kitchen of 10, William Black Street and I know it was in that room, in which it was difficult to move, that my mind first began to expand; and the atmosphere was revived for me the other night during a power cut.

CATHERINE COOKSON, FROM *LET ME MAKE MYSELF PLAIN –
A PERSONAL ANTHOLOGY*, 1988

Catherine Cookson

As Dame Catherine Cookson had already written at length about her philosophy in her book *Let Me Make Myself Plain – A Personal Anthology* she and I decided to include the same chapter in *The Relaxation Letters*.

THE AUTHOR

Henry Cooper, OBE, KSG

Former British Heavyweight Boxing Champion; Businessman

My personal way of relaxation and keeping fit is to be able to play golf whenever I have some free time and also relaxing with my family at home.

I am inspired by the following quotation:

Life without face is an arid business.

SIR NOEL COWARD

Joseph Corvo

World-Renowned Zone Therapist and Author

Many people ask me how I am able to remain so relaxed, energetic and vital when dealing with so many patients in a working day. The answer is that I practise the following meditation for 45 minutes at the beginning and end of each day:

I lie on the floor in a supine position, completely relaxed, with the telephone book under my head for the support of head and neck, and, do a prayer as follows:

The power of almighty God flows through me.

I think of nothing but those words during the entire meditation period, which completely recharges the physical, mental and spiritual bodies electromagnetically.

Everyone must have a goal to achieve in life, a mountain to climb. You must adjust your compass to arrive at your *port* on time and in safety.

Things to remember are:

You cannot help the poor by taking from the rich.
You should not do permanently for men things that men are able and capable of doing for themselves.

The following words say it all:

One ship drives East
And another drives West

Whilst the selfsame breezes blow.
Tis the set of the sails and *NOT*
The gales that bid them where to go.

God Bless.

Joseph Corvo

~~~~~~

Constance Cummings, CBE

American-born Actress

This is one of my favourite poems:

How happy is he born or taught,
That serveth not another's will;
Whose armour is his honest thought,
And simple truth his highest skill;

Whose passions not his masters are;
Whose soul is still prepared for death,
Untied unto the world with care
Of princes' grace or vulgar breath;

Who envies none whom chance doth raise,
Or vice; who never understood
The deepest wounds are given by praise,
By rule of state, but not of good;

Who hath his life from rumours freed;
Whose conscience is his strong retreat;
Whose state can neither flatterers feed,
Nor ruin make accusers great;

Who God doth late and early pray,
More of his grace than goods to send,
And entertains the harmless day
With a well-chosen book or friend –

This man is free from servile bands
Of hope to rise or fear to fall;

~~~~~~

Lord of himself, though not of lands;
And having nothing, yet hath all.

SIR HENRY WOTTON (1568–1639), 'THE CHARACTER OF A HAPPY LIFE'

The Dalai Lama XIV

Spiritual and Temporal Leader of Tibet, since 1940

The verse which has given me most inspiration in life is as follows:

> For as long as space endures,
> And for as long as living beings remain
> Until then may I, too, abide
> To dispel the misery of the world.

SHANTIDEVA, AN INDIAN BUDDHIST
SAINT

Pierre Daninos

French Author

I relax by playing tennis, listening to others, and having good meals.

My philosophy of life: If you have a bad day never look at the next day's enterprises with the eyes of the previous day.

I have found the following words a source of inspiration:

Do not take life too seriously; you will never get out of it alive.

E. HUBBARD

Geraldine Deaver

Retired Administrative Assistant (Banking)

Since I lost my husband, my life and reason for living have changed. What is helping me find my way and resume my life?

Most of all, the garden. There I work and relax, and, even in the winter when the weather is poor, I like to walk down the path of a morning when I let the cats out and just meander for a few minutes. A garden is a living entity and so must be cared for. My beloved cats are another of my important relaxants, and, as they are Siamese, we have some lively conversations. In the evening it is still a pleasure to prepare dinner, then eat my meal accompanied by some decent wine in front of the television. I also get a tremendous lift from certain operas – Puccini's *Tosca* and *Madame Butterfly*, Verdi's *La Traviata* and *Il Trovatore*, Tchaikovsky's *Eugene Onegin* and some of Wagner's *Ring*.

Nearly a year ago Audrey Burns Ross asked me if I would be willing to assist her with a project on which she was working. When she explained the idea and aims of this undertaking, I realized that this was the motivation I needed. While involved in the work, I found that many of the quotations and writings were having an inspiring and positive effect on me and were helping me as much as they had obviously been of help to the contributors.

My dear husband tried to instil into me two rules: never feel sorry for yourself and always be positive in your attitude towards everything life offers.

Dame Judi Dench, DBE, OBE

Actress (theatre, films and television)

To really relax, I like either to paint or sew.

There's a passage from *Hamlet* which has been a constant source of inspiration to me:

> . . . there's a special providence in the fall of a sparrow. If it be now, 'tis not to come; if it be not to come, it will be now; if it be not now, yet it will come – the readiness is all. Since no man owes of aught he leaves, what is't to leave betimes? Let be.

WILLIAM SHAKESPEARE (1564–1616), *HAMLET*, ACT V, SCENE i

The Late Monica Dickens, MBE

Writer; Founder of the Samaritans in Boston, Massachusetts 1974;
Great-Granddaughter of Charles Dickens

Here is a meditation which can be done with eyes open, while driving a car:

Settle your eyes on a fixed far-off point (tree, steeple etc.) and say aloud or to yourself:

There is a purpose to my existence.
I live, I love, I work, I die.
I am refreshed and begin life anew.

It works.

Author's note: Monica Dickens died in December 1992.

The Lady Dulverton

*Practitioner dealing with everything related to complementary
and vibrational medicine*

You ask for my comments on how I relax in life! An excellent question.

My philosophy is to 'keep going' with small breaks in between.

Although through complementary medicine, which as you know is what I practise, I concentrate continuously all day dowsing each patient – I find it *so* rewarding that in my own way it *is* relaxing!

Meditative and soft classical background music is another form of relaxation either before or at the end of a busy day. By meditative, I mean strengthening one's auras and filling them with God's beautiful white light, His love, His peace, His healing and His energies. This for me works wonders as only He can!

Another very positive way I have of relaxing is to swim my fifty lengths every morning. This clears out all the negative energies I collect daily in my aura. Riding is another way of grounding and earthing one's self and therefore a form of relaxation when riding through the beauty of nature.

It is essential to look around you on a daily basis and appreciate the 'positive' beauty there is around us and thank God for His wonders. Too many people transfer negative thought forms all day long and pity 'themselves' and their lives and their lot. However poor or ill one is, there is no point in thinking negatively as that is the way you really will end up.

Providing one is a 'giver' in life, God always ensures someone will give to you – often when you least expect anything.

There is a great deal of negativity about and many years ago my Mother gave me very good advice: 'Beware of splinters as you slide down the staircase of life.'

As I was well aware that splinters did exist, I ensured I avoided the negative aspects of life and have always done my utmost to be positive and relay positive thoughts to those around me. This doesn't *always* work but I still keep on trying to make a positive contribution to those around me and to this planet.

Find time to relax, live and let live. Nobody wants a misery around them.

I hope that this will help at least one person, then I'll be happy for them.

Anne Dunhill

Novelist; Italian Translator

My favourite way of relaxing is just going to bed. I feel great sympathy for those Victorian ladies who, worn out by giving birth to their large families, took to their beds with mysterious ailments and never got up again for the rest of their lives. Nowadays, if only doctors were imaginative enough to recommend it, it could be done in tremendous style. Without stirring from the bed one could shop by telephone, watch endless movies on TV, read voraciously and sip continuous champagne from a bedside fridge. I actually did once go to bed for a month with a threatened miscarriage. At first I felt terribly guilty that my husband, who was luckily on holiday, was waiting on me hand and foot, but at the end I really began to enjoy myself and thought nothing of sending him down two flights of stairs to fetch me some salt. The baby was saved, and the bond forged between my husband and myself by that episode can never be destroyed.

Sadly, all I can manage when the family are around are Sunday mornings in bed. We all have breakfast together – eating in bed gives me indigestion and crumbs – and then I climb back into bed with the newspapers for as long as the family will let me stay there. I'm quite convinced that it's these lazy Sunday mornings that enable me to cope with my week.

I make time for what I do – reading, writing, or translating – by working to a strict schedule. I count the days until my deadline and allocate myself so many pages per day. I also make sure that other – domestic or social – demands on my time are evenly spread out so they don't encroach on my working time. It's important to be able to say 'No, I can't do that today or tomorrow, but I will do it next week.' Obviously though something does have to go. In my case it's cooking. The family and I mainly eat raw foods, which are much better for us anyway. Several women have said to me, 'Oh I'd love to go to university / write a book if only I had time.' My answer, if I wasn't too tactful to make it, would be 'You do have time. You just happen to think making puff pastry's more important than reading the *Divina Commedia*.'

My antidote to stress is reading. However unhappy I am, my favourite authors can always transport me instantly into another world. I was famous, or perhaps I should say notorious, when my four children were small for being able to sit in their midst, totally lost in a book, while chaos and anarchy reigned around me.

As far as a philosophy of life goes, other people have said it much more beautifully than I could. I like T. S. Eliot's:

> And the end of all our exploring
> Will be to arrive where we started
> And know the place for the first time.

Drawing on my own personal experience I've come to the conclusion that women *can* have it all, but not all at once. By far the greatest formative experience of my life has been having children, and out of an expected life span of eighty years I can't understand why some women aren't prepared to devote five or ten years to their families. Quite apart from the child's needs, looking after small children is the greatest discipline and career training in the world. When you've done that you can do anything.

For my personal ambition, I'd like to be able to continue to learn for the rest of my life and not atrophy into a caricature of myself as many older people seem to. My ambition for the world is that everyone will one day have the right to painless birth and painless death. With all the other useless discoveries made by medical science, it seems strange that these first steps in human need haven't yet been mastered. For my

epitaph, which I'm trying to deserve though I don't yet, I'd like:
'Life didn't always smile at her, but she always smiled at life.'

Anne Dunhill

~~~~~~

H.S.H. Princess Elizabeth de Croÿ

*Her Serene Highness runs the animal welfare Refuge de Thiernay, France;
President, Defense et Protection des Animaux; Advisory Director of the
World Society for the Protection of Animals; apart from her work with
animals Her Serene Highness does a great deal of humanitarian work
throughout the world.*

My work is my relaxation, although I do find time occasionally to play
a game of Patience.

My philosophy of life is very much rooted in the philosophy of my
parents who believed that, if one is given great privilege, one must, in
turn, help others. They did this in a discreet way, and now, as I grow
older, I realize what a tremendous impression they made on me.

I believe we should devote time in our lives to other people, other
creatures. We owe it to them. After encountering great tragedies in the
world I became very aware of suffering, human and animal. This
prompted me to do more. Consequently I now devote my life to my
work, and never really know what is going to happen next. I am involved
seven days a week for fifty-two weeks of the year.

I am spiritually recharged by my work and it makes me feel very
happy to be able to help. I live in perpetual enchantment and look at
an animal as I would a work of art. The same applies when I see the
frightened face of a child who has suffered break into a smile.

*I believe relaxation and peace of mind can be achieved by doing something
one really believes in.*

In the end, we have all to account for what we have done, and, while
we are here on this earth, there is so much injustice to be tackled. My
great feeling is that we must share what we have and help in every
possible way we can by physically DOING SOMETHING.

Princess El. de Croÿ.

Bridge Ennis

Astrologer

How I relax – I dance.

My philosophy of life – To look to the night sky.

Some words which have inspired me (source unknown) –

Our human task is to learn lessons.
For this we are given a body.
Everything we need for our task
' is within our body.
Everyone we meet is a reflection
of our task.
Whatever we learn helps us
complete a lesson
And our lessons are repeated
till they're learnt.
Learning lessons doesn't end.
When one is learnt the next
presents itself.
This is our human task
For which we have a body
Which gives us what we need
To complete our task.

Sir Ranulph Fiennes, OBE

*Explorer and writer; part of the first unsupported crossing of the
Antartic land mass and the longest unsupported Polar journey
in Winter 1992–93*

I relax by having a hot bath and by going for a jog on Exmoor where
there are no people and no noise and no fumes, also by washing up
(the dishes).

My philosophy of life:
a) Introspection wastes time.
b) So does crying over spilt milk.
c) All is for the best in the best of all possible worlds,
   and, when it isn't . . . wait a bit and things will improve.

In the words of Burke: 'All that is necessary for the triumph of evil
is that good men do damn all.'

Shreela, The Baroness Flather

The first Asian woman to go to the House of Lords;
first Asian woman to hold the office of Mayor; first ethnic
minority woman councillor in the U.K.

I suppose I am like a great many women who try to combine at least three jobs in a day and sometimes I feel that the only 'relaxation' comes from changing one occupation for another! Of course it could not work all the time and I do have my very favourite ways of relaxing and unwinding.

Relaxation and unwinding are not the same thing. For unwinding I think it is very difficult to beat the box; nothing is guaranteed to empty the mind as completely as some series or old film on television. In fact the old black-and-white films are something which I enjoy enormously, I suppose mainly because some of them I can remember from the first time round. Yes I am that old! But also for the stylishness and the different era they evoke.

I love reading and mostly I read contemporary novels. The only trouble is that when the House is sitting there is so much paper to get through that I never get round to the current novel I have on the go. I quite often collect the books that I want to read and when I go on holiday I do almost nothing else except to lie in bed and read novels. For me that has to be the greatest luxury in life.

I would like to be able to go to the cinema much more than I do but by the time the end of the day or the end of the week comes I am just too tired physically to go to a film. This is something that I do miss very much because a film seen on the big screen is by no means the same as a film seen on the small screen.

The other thing which has helped me greatly and I almost call it my meditation is my swimming. I go three times a week and have a most enjoyable and relaxing time in the water. I love the feel of water, I always have done and find it very soothing.

I did some very hard thinking towards the end of last year and have realized that worrying about things which have not been done does not actually get them done. The only way for someone like me who has so many demands made on their time by so many people is to attempt to do as much as possible but without taking on the burden of guilt and creating anxiety.

In terms of personal philosophy I follow the basic principles stated in the *Gita*, the most important holy book of the Hindus, that one should do the right thing and one should put one's utmost effort in the doing, but one should not concern oneself with the result. It is enough in itself to have put all one's efforts into the doing – the result then is out of one's hands.

Bryan Forbes

Actor, Producer, Director, Writer

We will find life tolerable once we have consented to be always ill at ease.

GUSTAVE FLAUBERT (1821–80)

The Very Revd Graham Forbes

Provost, St Mary's Cathedral, Edinburgh

I relax and unwind principally by unwinding a trout or salmon line whilst up to my waist or chest, invariably in the freezing waters of the River Tay and virtually invariably without success. Catching or not catching has over the years almost become irrelevant. My favourite trout loch is at 1,000 feet, in the Perthshire hills; ospreys fly overhead, scanning the water in search of breakfast or tea. The trout are wild brown trout, 3 for 1lb, their firm pink flesh tastes delicious. My dog sits in the bow of the boat patiently waiting for either a fish to be landed or for me to pull ashore for a coffee break. What is magic about the place is that I'm in the middle of nowhere, I'm set against the elements of wind and rain, with a backdrop of bare timeless hills which will be there long after I'm gone.

My philosophy of life is best summed up in Salvador Dali's painting *Christ of St John of the Cross* (in Glasgow Art Gallery). The Christ is transfixed on the cross above his creation, arms permanently nailed apart, thus capable of receiving both love and rejection. I believe the Christian is challenged to be found at the foot of the Cross, being with the crucifieds of our day.

Graham Forbes

Anna Ford

BBC Television News Presenter and Journalist

I relax by learning to say no and not doing too much. It's important to have time to do nothing and to be spontaneous. If it's a nice day I'll go for a walk, or go and see a film at half an hour's notice with a good friend.

I also read and garden to relax.

Christina Foyle

Managing Director, W & G. Foyle Ltd;
began Foyle's Literary Luncheons in 1930

I relax by being with my animals and just stroking one of my fifteen cats soothes me, and looking at the peacocks, the most beautiful birds in the world, gives me joy.

My general philosophy of life is, if you are nice to people, they will be nice to you.

Two quotations have given me comfort:

There is no duty we so much underrate as the duty of being happy.
ARTHUR RANSOME (1884–1967)

A little health,
A little wealth,
A little house and freedom,
And at the end,
A little friend,
And little cause to need him.
SOURCE UNKNOWN

Christina Foyle

Clare Francis, MBE

Novelist and Former Yachtswoman

I relax and unwind by lying in the bath watching a good drama on television. I also have regular reflexology and aromatherapy, which is wonderfully indulgent. The British have a tradition of feeling guilty about self-indulgence of this sort, but I have no such problem. My general philosophy of life is to deal with each day as it comes, and to be thankful for it.

Dame Phyllis Frost, AC, DBE, CBE

Australian Vice Chairman Clean World International 1980–92;
Inaugural Chairman and Hon. Life Member of the Keep Australia
Beautiful Council; Trustee, Patron, Hon. Life Member, Hon. Convener and
Life Governor of many Community Service Organizations

HOW I RELAX AND UNWIND

Work is work only if there is something better that you want to do. I find nothing boring in my existence – I am a spiritually motivated woman so I do not get stressed. If I find I am being unduly concerned about things I still have my ability to pray and seek Divine guidance through Jesus Christ.

MY GENERAL PHILOSOPHY OF LIFE

I believe in the 30 Articles set down in the Universal Declaration of Human Rights. I hold a reverence for life no matter where I find it, believing that souls have no colour, and everybody is equal in the eyes of God. My reverence for life also covers all living things, including animals, birds, fish and plants. If it is necessary for me to use them, e.g., for food, shelter or any other reason, I do so, but I never involve myself in excess of any commodities. I believe to justify one's own existence one is duty bound to serve and assist activities that go towards creating and maintaining a healthier life-style for the planet and those things that live upon it. I have made a conscious endeavour to develop the heart of a lion, the hide of a rhinoceros, and tenacity and courage which cannot easily be downed.

I cannot answer this because there is so much that has been written not only in the Bible but in many other volumes which has guided me a great deal, but perhaps I should finish off with a small poem.

I have to live with myself, and so
I want to be fit for myself to know,
I want to be able, as days go by,
Always to look myself straight in the eye;
I don't want to stand, with the setting sun,
And hate myself for things I have done.

I can never hide myself from me;
I see what others may never see;
I know what others may never know,
I never can fool myself, and so,
Whatever happens, I want to be
Self-respecting and conscience free.

EDGAR A. GUEST, 'MYSELF',

FIRST AND LAST VERSES

David Gee

Husband, Father, Part-Time Consultant in Environmental and
· Occupational Risk; TV Presenter and Author; Former Director of
Friends of the Earth

I am afraid that I find very little time to relax and when I do it is usually
in a bath with a gin and tonic following a three-mile run round
Wandsworth Common, which I live next to. Being armed with the twin
philosophies of *Carpe Diem* ('Seize the day') and 'Each day is the first
day of the rest of your life' means that I am always trying to pack as
much into each day as possible.

Since getting a dog a year ago I now cycle round the Common with
it for 20 minutes each day and I find that very relaxing.

Bob Geldof, KBE

Singer, Songwriter, Producer; Initiator and Organizer of Band Aid,
Live Aid and Sport Aid fund-raising events

I relax and unwind by reading, playing music, watching telly, walking, sleeping.

My philosophy of life: Do it.

My favourite quotation: 'The best ideals put into practice become merely politics' – Gorbachev, I think.

A poem that has inspired me:

Out of Ireland have we come.
Great hatred, little room,
Maimed us at the start.
I carry from my mother's womb
A fanatic heart.

W. B. YEATS (1865–1939),

'REMORSE FOR INTEMPERATE SPEECH', LAST VERSE

Peter Gellhorn, FGSM

*Conductor and Chorus Master Glyndebourne Festival Opera 1954–61,
rejoined music staff 1974 and 1975; Professor, Guildhall School of Music
and Drama since 1981*

For relaxation I like walking, occasionally swimming, and going to plays.

I feel that it is important to enjoy the good things that human beings do, while being aware that we do many terrible things too. As time goes on I have had less and less time for Messiahs, Gurus, etc., finding that decent people have always been decent without them, and that the others do not change their ways, despite hypocritical protestations.

I have been inspired by the worlds of Polonius in Shakespeare's *Hamlet*: 'To thine own self be true.'

Peter Gellhorn.

Susan George

International Actress and Producer

I relax and unwind by spending time with and loving my dogs.

My general philosophy of life is to live for each day.

My inspiration comes from the poem by Robert Browning, *Rabbi ben Ezra:* 'The best is yet to be.'

First verse of the poem –

Grow old along with me!
The best is yet to be,
The last of life, for which the first was made:
Our times are in His hands
Who saith 'a whole I planned,
Youth shows but half; trust God: see all, nor be afraid!'

Sir Alexander Gibson, Kt, CBE

Founder 1962 and Music Director, 1985–87, Scottish Opera
(Artistic Director 1962–85); Conductor Laureate since 1987

In the reverse order of your questions, a quote from Rachmaninov has from time to time reassured me that it is not altogether unhealthy to be obsessed with one subject – sometimes to the exclusion of all other concerns and aspects of life. He is quoted on the sleeve of a recording of his 2nd Symphony by Eugene Ormandy and the Philadelphia Orchestra:

> I am myself only in music,
> Music is enough for a whole lifetime –
> but a lifetime is not enough for music.

So I suppose my general philosophy of life consists of accepting the fact that music means more to me than any other facet of life and I count myself indeed fortunate that it can be my relaxation as well as my occupation, my consolation in times of stress and my inspiration in facing up to the vicissitudes of life.

I am also fortunate in having a wife and four children who accept this state of affairs and back me up without question or reservation.

I read scores for relaxation – especially scores of music I don't have to prepare for an imminent performance – but I also read books, mostly history and biography.

Generally, however, I am myself only in music and I believe almost Calvanistically, especially as a conductor who depends upon others who in turn are largely dependent on him, that a conductor's work is never done. There are always new scores to learn but I find I spend more and more time on the scores I think I have known for decades. No lifetime is long enough for a servant of music, but I never cease to wonder at the achievement of the composers whose lifespans were so tragically short. It is indeed a privilege to serve all of them by being involved in the process which keeps their music alive.

Sir John Gielgud, CH

International Actor

It has taken all the long years of my career to learn to find a way to relax, and film and television seem to demand a new problem different from what one has discovered in stage acting. Instinct and experiment are the only qualities I have gradually come to rely on, and I don't really think one can lay down any rules. Everything depends on one's diligence and self-criticism, and everyone has to find out for themselves how to cope with the difficulties.

John Gielgud.

Graham Gooch, OBE

British Cricketer

I relax and unwind by being at home with the children. I am not able to see them very much, but when I do I enjoy their company. They help me to relax from the pressures of international sport and I often go for walks in the nearby forest with the family. I also enjoy listening to music.

My philosophy of life is to give of my best in everything I do, in sport, in everyday life – sometimes I fail horribly – and to help others achieve their potential in cricket, especially my team mates at Essex and my England colleagues. I am thankful for the talent that I have, which enables me to see the world and to witness how the other half live.

Sorry, I'm not into poetry.

Carolyn Grace

Aviator; the only woman in the world currently flying a Spitfire

I now, in my widowhood, find relaxation no longer is tied with unwinding so to speak. Relaxation for me is to take flight in either the Stampe, a 1936 biplane, or the Spitfire Mark IX T, which my late husband Nick Grace restored single-handedly to flying condition from 1980–85.

I find it so exhilarating to leave the confines and complexities of Mother Earth behind and experience the freedom of the air around us – playing chase with the softness of the summer clouds, or tackling the mirth of the tormented winter sky. The sheer unadulterated pleasure of flying, coupled with sense of achievement, is uplifting and inspiring. The concentration required, particularly in the Spitfire, is so intense that all other problems are put aside. The feeling of apprehension mixed with great expectations is a powerful cocktail which never lessens with experience, for with experience comes the challenge to perfect and to pursue further the countless realms that flying has to offer.

To unwind is a very rare commodity. The great responsibilities that I now have make it apparent that the risks involved in unwinding and letting one's defences down exclude the pleasure.

My philosophy is to go forward, to drive onwards in unison with the past gaining as much information from past experiences as I can. I feel that one can gain from each day our material for a better future. To not realize this fact is not to make full use of our lives for ourselves, our children and our world.

My husband Nick often said that 'life was not a rehearsal' and I have found these words have been a continual inspiration to me.

Billy Graham

American Evangelist

BEAUTIFUL HOME AND GARDENS

When Spring comes to our mountain home, my wife heads for the garden. She has always kept a home of comfort and beauty for our family. When I am in yet another hotel room in some city around the world, I often think of our mountain home, filled with a lifetime of memories and love.

Imagine some of the most beautiful places in the world. Switzerland when the sun breaks over the snow-capped peaks and spills onto the slopes filled with wild flowers. A crystal clear lake, nestled among pine trees. A beach with white sand and the gentle lapping of the warm Caribbean waters. A night in the desert west with a million stars against a velvet backdrop. An Autumn day on a quiet road in New England. An easy chair, a good book, a cup of hot chocolate, and a glowing fire when the snow is falling at home.

Heaven will be more than that, because it is the Father's house, and He is a God of beauty. The same hand that made the beauty of this world has a more beautiful place prepared for us.

Man has polluted so much of our earth, but in Heaven there will be no environmental concerns. The water will be pure, the air clean, and there will be no need for landfills or recycled paper and cans.

In Revelation, when John caught a glimpse of Heaven, the only thing he could think to compare it to was a bride on her wedding day. I have three daughters and two daughters-in-law, and every one was a beautiful bride, but their beauty was just a dim reflection of Heaven.

If we are amazed and thrilled when we view some of the beauty the

Lord gave us on earth, I'm sure we are in for some wonderful surprises in Heaven.

Today, more than ever, we need to know how to find strength to live life to its fullest.

Too often we neglect the privilege of prayer until we encounter suffering or difficulty.

Comfort and prosperity have never enriched the world as much as adversity has done.

A keen sense of humor helps us to overlook the unbecoming, understand the unconventional, tolerate the unpleasant, overcome the unexpected, and outlast the unbearable.

No matter how dark and hopeless a situation might seem, never stop praying.

Author's note: The above are extracts from Dr Graham's book, *Hope for the Troubled Heart* published by Word, Inc., Dallas, Texas. Copyright 1991 by Billy Graham.

Due to confidentiality agreements between Word, Inc., and Billy Graham his signature cannot appear in this publication.

Dr Vartan Gregorian

The President, Brown University, Rhode Island, USA;
an Armenian, born in Tabriz, Iran

Relaxation for me takes the form of a late repose on a Sunday morning. Other times are those isolated evenings when nothing is scheduled. Otherwise, I lead a pretty hectic life.

My approach to life and my beliefs are very much rooted in the influence and philosophy of my maternal grandmother. She was one of my greatest teachers and a most remarkable woman.

Her influence was tremendous. She had no formal education, but immensely valued it. She lived her life with consummate dignity. She struggled. She coped. She never lost faith, was never cynical. She did not speak ill of others. She insisted that one must do good without expectation of reward. She believed that to think ill of others is to diminish oneself.

One of the many things she taught me was that dignity is not negotiable. Dignity is the honour of the family. I have thought about it many times.

She also taught me that envy is very bad. Envy will deform your character. 'You must not have a hole in your eye', she would say. The hole in the eye was caused by envy. The hole would be insatiable and could never be filled.

She knew about the evil eye and believed in it. 'You do not show your baby to someone with the evil eye!'

In 1947, when the opportunity presented itself for me to continue my education in Beirut my father tried to dissuade me and was dead set against the idea. My grandmother, however, and I remember it so clearly, said very calmly, 'I would like my son to go and become a man. To become a man, he needs an education.'

I left for Beirut when I was fifteen, with fifty dollars in my pocket. I began my studies at the College Arménien. That was a turning point in my life.

I believe: 'that teachers are governed by three things. One, they must be enthusiastic. Two, they must remember that the student has never heard any of this before. And, three, they must tell the truth. Above all, the truth.

I consider: 'Ignorance is a sin as it deprives the individual of knowledge and autonomy, and dignity. Education, learning and scholarship constitute acts of faith in the continuity of humanity. They honour the past and serve as a witness to the future. And after all, the business of education is the creation of the future.'

QUOTATION

One of mine, which I have recently used in an introductory speech, is, 'Universities and museums are the DNA of society.'

The Rt. Hon. The Lord Hanson

Chairman Hanson PLC since 1965; Hanson Transport Group Ltd since 1965

Leonardo da Vinci wrote: 'Every now and then go away, relax a little, then, when you come back to work, your judgement will be surer'

My own day must have been productive before I can relax. For a businessman, there's always *something* to be done before the end of every day, especially at home. Only if I completely 'clear my desk', which of course means different things to different people, can I truly relax.

The knowledge that I have done something positive means that when I unwind, I feel I have deserved it. Relaxation is always more valuable after real achievement.

Most of all, to be able to relax is to keep life well organized but simple. As in *Richard III:* 'An honest tale speeds best being plainly told.'

Sir John Harvey-Jones, MBE

Chairman of Parallax Enterprises Ltd.

One of the ways that I do, in fact, control stress is by trying to avoid taking on more than I can handle!

John Harvey-Jones

Sir Michael Hordern, CBE

Actor

I go fishing.

Michael Hordern

Bishop Trevor Huddleston, CR

St James's Church, Piccadilly, London

I just don't really do anything except find maximum enjoyment and purpose with every day, and the realization that time for these things gets shorter and shorter.

+ Trevor Huddleston. CR.

Sir Peter Imbert, QPM

Retired as Commissioner of the Metropolitan Police in January 1993;
this contribution was written when serving as Commissioner

When I was appointed to my post as Commissioner of Police of the Metropolis – one of the largest police services in the western world – I recognized that during my term of office there was likely to be little opportunity for me to relax fully and please myself in any free time that I might have. Although I must give my full attention to the Service, and thereby the people of London, it is true that the pressure of all work and no play would not be good for me either mentally or physically, nor would it be helpful to those I am endeavouring to serve – either the public or my own colleagues.

I do play some rather poor golf but my standard of play merely exchanges one set of frustrations for another! My family is my relaxation. I am fortunate to have three children, two of whom are now married and have presented my wife and me with three lovely grandchildren – and there is little which is more relaxing or more fun than trying to teach a three-year-old boy to play cricket.

My eldest sister said that one should try and leave this world a better place than it was when one entered it. She lived that way and, although she died young, her wisdom and gentility have, for me, been an enduring example.

Another plank of my philosophy of life is to turn disadvantage to advantage and to do this with cheerfulness, always with courtesy but, where appropriate, with firmness and determination. There are times for every one of us when everything seems to be going wrong. Life can be unkind, but it is also true that every cloud has a silver lining. My philosophy for the police service has been to endeavour to provide a fair, firm and friendly organization. In the face of crisis this is seldom an easy task but I have a personal motto (one of many!) that today's crisis is tomorrow's history – provided you handle today's problems properly!

I learnt Rudyard Kipling's poem 'If' by heart when I was about seven years old, but little did I know how much the words and the philosophy behind them would sustain me in my career, particularly when the going got very tough.

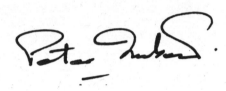

Jeremy Irons

International Oscar-Winning Actor

I relax and unwind by partaking in solitary pleasures such as walking with my dog, horse riding, gardening, sailing and ski-ing.

In broad terms my philosophy of life is to think very carefully before I choose what to aim for, and then put all my energies in that direction.

A quotation which has for a long time been in the back of my mind:

Come to the edge
It is too high
Come to the edge
We might fall
Come to the edge
And they came
And he pushed them
And they flew.

GUILLAUME APOLLINAIRE (1880–1918)

Glenda Jackson, MP

Member of Parliament and former Oscar-Winning Actress

A simple quotation which I have always found to be apt throughout my life is 'Only connect' (E. M. Forster).

Glenda Jackson.

Cornelis de Jager

Netherlands Astronomer

I have several, equally pleasant ways of relaxing and unwinding. One of these is doing scientific research, an activity that I find emotionally relaxing and very distracting. The other way is jogging, including participating in official long-distance running competitions. This is an activity so far away from my daily life that it helps to see problems in their appropriate perspective.

My philosophy of life: I believe that the two greatest achievements of our western culture during the last millennium are the developments of democracy and of modern science. Both are footed on the same philosophy of life. They require impartial judgment, they need a critical and mature spirit, they demand consideration, debate and acceptance of other opinions. Developing, preserving and defending these achievements is an obligation that I find most important.

Quotation: 'Cogito, ergo sum' (Cartesius: I think, hence I exist).

Derek Jameson

News, Television and Radio Commentator and Presenter

I am a fatalist who goes where the wind takes me. My Sagittarian birth, perhaps, or could it be a philosophy adopted in those early years when I grew up in the East End without the benefit of parents, often begging money on the streets to buy bread?

The angels have always looked after me. Ma Wren, the old lady who lived in a shoe and raised more than seventy waifs and strays like myself, always touched my cleft chin when I was feeling low and would say: 'You'll be all right. You're touched by the angels!'

And so I was. At the age of 14, I took myself off to Fleet Street and got a job as a messenger boy. From that inauspicious start I went on to edit four national newspapers and then became a star of radio and television. The author and critic, Auberon Waugh reckons I am the best-known person in Britain – so the kid from a backstreet slum did quite well.

My recipe for success: to be absolutely sure what it is you want to do, to master your subject to the very best of your ability and then go for it with total dedication and enthusiasm. It helps to be lucky.

Brush aside stress and worry. If you slip down the ladder, grit your teeth and start climbing up all over again.

I'm not much good at relaxation, as you will have gathered, though I do confess to playing opera at full blast (away from the neighbours) to blot out anxious moments. A couple of hours of Pavarotti and Domingo is the perfect remedy for all that ails mankind.

Surgeon Commander Rick Jolly, OBE, Royal Navy

I find it easy to relax and unwind. I just sit down and fall asleep for ten minutes. Catnapping is a useful art, learned as a houseman at Barts, often used since – and especially useful during war!

If pressed, and unable to sleep, I like listening to the singer Enya through portable CD headphones!

My philosophy of life: The spark of life does not become extinct after death, but the 'spirit'/'animus' passes on to another dimension or phase which is inadequately described by the words Heaven and Hell. Human language is inadequate and our brains too small to comprehend but a glimpse of this.

> The Moving Finger writes; and, having writ,
> Moves on: nor all thy Piety nor Wit
>   Shall lure it back to cancel half a Line,
> Nor all thy Tears wash out a Word of it . . .
>
> Ah Love! could thou and I with Fate conspire
> To grasp this sorry Scheme of Things entire,
>   Would not we shatter it to bits – and then
> Re-mould it nearer to the Heart's Desire!

TWO VERSES FROM *THE RUBÁIYÁT* BY OMAR KHAYYÁM

(?1050–1123; TRANSLATED BY EDWARD FITZGERALD)

Deborah Kerr

International Actress; Stage, Films and Television

I relax and unwind in the garden of my house here in Spain or outside on the terrace of my home in Switzerland. I have utter peace and quiet in both places and I enjoy reading a book, or merely watching my cats play and listening to the songs of the birds. If the weather is vile, I relax by watching sport of any kind on television!

My general philosophy of life would have to be: 'Never make heavy weather of things' – advice from my aunt who, at forty-seven, unexpectedly produced her first child!

The Serenity Prayer is my constant inspiration:

'God grant me the Serenity to accept the things I cannot change, Courage to change the things I can and Wisdom to know the difference.'

REINHOLD NIEBUHR

Glenys Kinnock

Board Member of UNICEF UK, on its behalf visited Sudan 1992;
addressed special meeting of UN concerning the children of South Africa;
Chair of One World and One World Action

I relax either by reading a novel, or by going to the cinema or theatre.
A poem that has been an inspiration to me is this one by W. H.
Auden:

There will be no peace.
Fight back, then, with such
courage as you have
And every unchivalrous dodge
you know of,
clear in your conscience on this:
Their cause, if they had one, is
nothing to them now;
They hate for hate's sake.

W. H. AUDEN (1907–73), 'THERE WILL BE NO PEACE'

The Rt. Hon. Neil Kinnock, MP

Leader of the British Labour Party 1983–92

They walked this road in seasons past
When all the skies were overcast,
They breathed defiance as they went
Along those troubled hills of Gwent.

They talked of justice as they strode
Along this crooked mountain road,
And dared the little Lords of Hell
So that the future should be well.

Because they did not count the cost
But battled on when all seemed lost,
This empty ragged road shall be
Always a sacred road to me.

IDRIS DAVIES, 'THE SACRED ROAD'

Helmut Kohl

Chancellor of Germany

Because of my many duties I have very little free time. I spend most of it with my family and enjoy walking in the Pfalzer forest. I also enjoy reading, particularly biographies and books with historical themes.

For the last 22 years I have spent my holidays in St Gilgen on the Wolfgangsee in the Salzburg District of Austria. I spend my time there swimming and walking in the mountains.

The first Chancellor of the German Federal Republic, Konrad Adenauer, once said something which I particularly treasure. He said, 'Freedom carries with it obligations.' These words are the theme of my political work.

Wim Kok

Deputy Prime Minister and Minister of Finance, The Netherlands

In our country it seems to be a rare occasion for the Minister of Finance and Deputy Prime Minister to get a moment of rest at all. Working days of sixteen hours or more are no exception in this profession. This is ironic because, in my work, I am trying to get a larger share of the population back to working life again. Though I suppose in my job timesharing isn't really feasible, I do sense a need for more equality in employment opportunities.

On the other hand I think it would be fair to say that working hard fits well into my general philosophy of life. Now that the Cold War is over at last and the end of ideology is proclaimed, we all too often witness a kind of fatigue when confronted with the need to tackle the problems of the modern world. There is so much to be done to reduce social injustice, to improve the standard of life in developing countries, to enhance the quality of the environment, etc.! So from that point of view I believe there is much to say for seeing a rewarding challenge in a hard day's work.

The few hours I have to spare I prefer to spend with my family; watching a good football match on television is a favourite pastime. During holidays I like to go out camping and enjoy nature or visit cultural sights.

The Rt. Hon. Ian Lang, MP

The Secretary of State for Scotland

The quotation which I would like to offer you is one which has given me a great deal of thought over the years, from Edmund Burke:

> I am not one of those who think that the people are never in the wrong. They have been so, frequently and outrageously, both in other countries and in this. But I do say, that in all disputes between them and their rulers, the presumption is at least upon a par in favour of the people.

EDMUND BURKE (1729–97), 'THOUGHTS ON THE CAUSE
OF THE PRESENT DISCONTENTS' (1770)

Jane Lapotaire

Actress

I relax and unwind by three methods. By hill walking in the Cotswolds, the Peak District or preferably Cumbria; by zonking myself into unconsciousness with half a bottle of wine and sleeping in the sun; and I also meditate twice a day, choosing a meditation that suits my needs at the time, i.e. health meditation, spiritual meditation, affirmations. I have no general philosophy of life, as life has a way of challenging whatever the last definition was that you made about it. I can only say I see it as a learning journey and am deeply grateful for all the blessings I have in my life.

A journey of a thousand miles begins with a single step.

Jane Lapotaire

Julian Lloyd Webber

'Cellist

I like to relax and unwind by doing something which has nothing to do with music. This can mean anything from meeting friends (who are often non-musicians) in a pub or restaurant, reading something which has nothing to do with music (dark fantasy and black humour are two current favourites), going to a football match (I'm a Leyton Orient supporter) or just walking and spending as much time as possible in the countryside.

All the while, of course, my subconscious is living with music, but I personally find it essential in such a pressurized profession physically to remove myself from music and its surroundings on a regular basis in order to retain my sanity and perspective.

Different words or phrases can be an inspiration at different times but I would like to select two now:

Be in this world, but not of it.
What is the use of running if you are not on the right road?

The Rt. Hon. The Earl of Longford, KG, PC

I feel that I am rather an imposter in offering thoughts about relaxation and life. I would much rather hear the views of others, including yourself. You have told me that I ought to try closing my eyes and concentrating on my breathing. I will gladly do so but I expect that I shall take time to benefit.

I have recently emerged from hospital after an operation following a heavy fall. Everyone says to me, 'you musn't do too much, you must rest, you must relax'. It all sounds fine, unless and until you have to do it. A little while ago I should have found no difficulty about your question regarding relaxation. I have led, I suppose, what would be called a very active life (mentally) as University Teacher, Cabinet Minister, Banker, Publisher and Social Worker. If you had asked me how I relaxed in the course of all these activities, I should have mentioned that I usually spend the weekend writing books (a score or so) and in physical exercise. With the passing of the years, the latter has become much feebler, but (again until recently) I was jogging (very slowly) at weekends. The fact that I have been supported for sixty years by a remarkable wife (eight children, twenty-six grandchildren, three great-grandchildren) has provided, I suppose, an alternative to an official policy of relaxation.

But now, for the time being at least, as mentioned above, I have got to go slow and relax. I cannot pretend that I am finding it at all easy. There is a religious approach which appeals to me strongly. I have just been reading an extremely helpful book by Delia Smith, known to everyone as a leading cookery writer, but admired by me for her religious message. I can quote only one sentence: 'Being receptive to God means allowing Him to work in His way and at His speed.' There is much more in expansion of that guidance.

Not long ago, I wrote a book on *Suffering* in which some noble contemporary sufferers explained how they united their sufferings with those of Christ on the Cross.

For most of us such aspirations seem almost beyond our power to fulfil. But at least for Christians and non-Christians alike the idea of *willing acceptance* alike of pleasure and pain provides an essential clue.

French
England

Dr Tom Burns McArthur

English Teacher since 1959; Feature Writer since 1962;
Lecturer and Writer on Yoga and Indian Philosophy since 1962;
Author and Language Consultant since 1970; Editor, English Today *since*
1984; Oxford Companion to the English Language since 1987

I think Patanjali probably got it right in India over two thousand years ago. 'Still the ripples of the mind,' he said, and wrote a little classic of yoga about how (maybe) to do it. I'm still working on those ripples. Rhythmic breathing helps a bit, but not when the ripples become tidal waves of sorrow or fear. Sometimes just getting things down to ripple size is achievement enough. Very occasionally things do go beautifully still and clear. Usually when least expected.

Tom McArthur

Feri McArthur

Yoga Teacher; Managing Editor the Oxford Companion to the English Language

You asked me about my general philosophy of life. There is no simple answer to this question.

Generally I work hard towards achieving my goals without expecting any help on the way or any results at the end. Consequently if my efforts bear fruit I am delighted, and if not I shrug and move on to the next goal.

Hamish MacInnes, OBE, BEM

Founder and Leader, Glencoe Mountain Rescue Team since 1960;
Author and Film Consultant, BBC and major movies; Director,
Glencoe Productions Ltd since 1989; Hon. Director Leishman Memorial
Research Centre, Glencoe since 1975

I find being in mountains or by the sea my ideal way of relaxing; this together with an interest in yoga during my teens has enabled me to relax very easily, even in stressful situations.

It has been my aim, not always successfully I must admit, to try to conduct my life by treating others as I would like to be treated and I feel that one should contribute, even in the most humble way, in helping others. I have been fortunate in being able to do this as a mountaineer in the field of mountain rescue, but this seems inadequate when compared to those who year after year look after the needs of the old and infirm.

Over the years I have had inspiration from many poems, and books of verse were always part of my swag even in the most remote regions. Lines from Flecker's *Hassan* often seemed appropriate for my travels.

> We travel not for trafficking alone;
>   By hotter winds our fiery hearts are fanned:
> For lust of knowing what should not be known,
>   We take the Golden Road to Samarkand.

JAMES ELROY FLECKER (1884–1915), *HASSAN*, V, ii

Virginia McKenna

Actress; Trustee, the Born Free Foundation

What is the Earth?
A ball in space?
A little paradise?
Planet of melting ice
And inner fires?

Under my hand
Its surface crumbles
Crushed underfoot
Its myriad flowers.

Forests lie trembling
Under my sword
The ocean darkens
Weeping black tears.

Death of sweet rivers
Death-giving rain
Silent and secret
Invisible pain.

A gift from heaven
This little world
Each bird a jewel
Each tree a mother.

What is the Earth?
A fragile heart.
Tender my touch
To save its life –
And mine.

VIRGINIA McKENNA, 'WHAT IS THE EARTH?' (1991)

~~~~~~~~

Clare Maxwell-Hudson

Major international figure in Health, Massage, Beauty Therapy and Education; Director, The Institute of Health Sciences, London; Author

I'm in the extremely lucky position that my main form of relaxation is also my job.

To me, giving a massage is as therapeutic and relaxing for the giver as it is for the receiver. It could be called active meditation. The rhythm of the movements can be so soothing and hypnotic that you feel as though you are floating; everything seems effortless and relaxed. By concentrating on the rhythm of the massage you become absorbed in what you are doing and when you finish you are as refreshed and revitalized as your client. What a wonderful job.

My philosophy is to do with attitude: I think that you should try to get things done rather than talking and agonizing about them – this helps to prevent anxiety. I also think one should try and keep things as simple as possible and to try to enjoy everything one does.

Another marvellous way to relax is to sit and watch a cat relax. As Montaigne said, 'Have you known how to take repose? You have done more than he who has taken cities and empires.'

This is another of my favourite quotations:

Saints and kings, prophets and dervishes, all bow down before beauty, descending from the unknown world.
We love beauty because it is not merely of this Earth: beauty in the human being is a reflection of celestial beauty itself.

MAHMUD SHABISTARI: *SECRET GARDEN,*
SUFI WRITING OF THE 13th CENTURY

Clare Maxwell-Hudson.

94

Dame Jean Maxwell-Scott, DCVO

Lady-in-Waiting to HRH Princess Alice, Duchess of Gloucester, since 1959

When I get home to Scotland, tired and stiff, after a long drive from the South, I enjoy an ecstatic welcome from the dogs; then, if it is the right time of day, I go down to the stables to feed the horses and hens. I find this most unwinding – there is something soothing about feeding animals and seeing that their stables are comfortable for the night and the hens are safe from foxes.

Other things I find relaxing are arranging flowers, doing some not-too-violent gardening, reading and listening to music.

We are so lucky to live at Abbotsford with a house full of books, a garden full of flowers and room to keep animals. The house is open to the public, so hopefully our visitors enjoy them too.

When I get to Carter Bar on my way home and see Scotland spreading before me I always think of:

> Breathes there the man with soul so dead,
> Who never to himself hath said,
> This is my own, my native land!
> Whose heart hath ne'er within him burn'd,
> As home his footsteps he hath turn'd
> From wandering on a foreign strand!
> If such there breathe, go, mark him well;
> For him no minstrel raptures swell;
> High though his titles, proud his name;
> Boundless his wealth as wish can claim;
> Despite those titles, power, and pelf,
> The wretch, concentred all in self,
> Living, shall forfeit fair renown,

And, doubly dying, shall go down
To the vile dust, from whence he sprung,
Unwept, unhonour'd, and unsung.

WALTER SCOTT (1771–1832), FROM 'THE LAY OF THE LAST MINSTREL',

CANTO SIXTH (I)

Jean Maxwell-Scott.

Author's note: Sir Walter Scott died at Abbotsford on 21 September 1832; Dame Jean is a direct descendant.

June Mendoza, RP, ROI

*Artist, who has painted many international figures including
H.M. The Queen. Her large group paintings include* The House of
Commons in Session, *1986 and the* House of Representatives
for the new Parliament building in Canberra

Space for relaxation? Hard to find.

Apart from large doses of theatre and music of all kinds, there is the evening bean bag (The Nest) where, gawping (often witlessly) at TV, I sew – needlepoint, patchwork; read; knit; sort out and arrange the constant flow of my photographs of daily events, etc.; and generally decrease the momentum of the day.

Sunday is, when possible, kept tightly hugged to ourselves and the family, and also when I get mind-blocked and ratty with those Sunday business phone intrusions.

Philosophy of life? I must have one. I certainly have a code within which I have to live comfortably with myself.

In my lectures I mutter things like Integrity, Discipline and Quality. That's about painting but it's all one and the same really. You get a blank canvas, fill it to the best of your abilities, honesty, energy and experience. You accept the inevitable resulting flaw (your own of course); you have to or you wouldn't start the next canvas, and that's unthinkable.

There's also this funny thing of playing fair with the gods. I know if I don't they've immediately and triumphantly *got* me. If you do, there's that warm relationship out of which come all sorts of goodies – like serenity and confidence.

Superstition? Conscience? A code?

Communication. I love communication and it's amazing what

happens because of it.

I don't know. Working hard. Trying. What else?

My favourite quotations:

'If' – Kipling.

'A Talent should be returned in better order than when received' – my mother.

Do it. Don't waste a moment. If it hurts anyone else in any way, don't do it.

June Mendoza

Michael Meyer

Biographer and Translator

I relax by going to sleep (anywhere, anytime), and watching any sport except motor racing.

My philosophy of life is to have limited ambitions.

Keith Michell

Actor; Artist; Author

I have certainly found that general health and state of mind and spirit are affected by the food I eat – and Macrobiotics seems to be the most satisfactory solution to eating. It has helped me for many years now to cope with the rigours of theatre and life.

Macrobiotics is a practical way of selecting, preparing and cooking whole foods and is based on the ancient concept of Tao – of Yin and Yang – the complementary opposites which together make the whole. Food has its opposites, its acids and alkalines, which can help find balance in diet.

When I started eating this way it meant a menu, surprisingly varied, of whole grains, beans, vegetables and some fish flavoured with soy sauce, miso, sesame and malted syrups. It was a whole new world of delicacies, excluding sugar products and junk foods. The result was immediate weight loss and a feeling of relaxation – a sort of 'high' you might say, only it was kicking the 'drugs' (sugars, caffeines, chemical additives and such) which led to a lack of stress – call it happiness – I hadn't experienced in years.

You are what you eat. Eat what you feel like, but always remember Yin and Yang.

It could, as some suggest, be all in the mind. Yin and Yang, though is being integrated firmly into Western philosophy. The spirit of Macrobiotics – the oneness of Man, Nature and the Universe – seems to be surviving.

Bishop Hugh Montefiore

Author, Writer, former Bishop of Birmingham;
Chairman Friends of the Earth Trust

I have found that the best antidote to stress is to keep a quiet time in my chapel in the morning before breakfast, when I have a period of meditation and contemplation in the presence of God. This starts me off refreshed and relaxed at the beginning of the day. I did not do it in order to avoid stress, but I find that on occasions when I miss out on it I feel much more stressed. I hope this doesn't sound too pietistic: it just happens to be true for me. During the day, the best antidote to stress is to concentrate totally on the people you meet or the work you are doing: then you don't look back with remorse or look forward with worry; you are too engrossed in the present. I used to have a large notice stuck up on the office board when I was Vicar of the civic and university church of Great St Mary's Cambridge, where crises seemed to come thick and fast. It read: NOTHING REALLY MATTERS. Not 'nothing matters' because it does, but in the perspective of eternity it is true that nothing really matters and it was good to be reminded of this from time to time. I find that I cannot work after supper. If I do, I just cannot get to sleep until 3 a.m. – the mind goes on revving up – so if I have a lot of work to do, I get up early, 5 a.m. sometimes, but whatever happens I relax with a book or with TV or with gossip in the evening.

As for my philosophy of life, I am a Christian, so I really do believe that when I make a mistake I can be forgiven and there is nothing therefore basically to worry about. Things are what they are, and their consequences will be what they will be. As Paul wrote, 'all things work together for good for those that love God' – even the bad things! As for the future, grace is always available to help one to cope, and things usually turn out better than one fears. The future is a challenge which can wait until it comes. It is better to concentrate on the here and now. I do believe in the 'sacrament of the present moment'. The present moment contains all the challenge, the excitement, the stimulus, and the grace that I need. Real life is meeting, and one meets people and things not in the future or the past, but the present.

There are two Scriptural texts which I have always found a help in addition to my motto: 'Nothing really matters'. One comes from the Gospels: 'Take no thought for the morrow, for the morrow will take care for the things of itself' (Matt. 6.34). And another is from the writings of St Paul: 'My grace is sufficient for thee; for my strength is made perfect in weakness' (2 Corinthians 12.9). Together, I find they banish stress.

Roger Moore

International Actor; Ambassador for UNICEF

I truly love a long, hot soak in the bath. It is my one chance to catch up on my reading without anyone interfering and whoever gets the newspapers after me finds they are very soaked.

This confines me to reading the tabloids because you cannot read the broadsheets in the bath.

Frederick Muller

International Film Production Executive

Many years ago I did nothing but work, work, work, without thinking much about my health and my social life. My family was always on the forefront of my thoughts, but they too were sacrificed at times for the sake of my professional activities. Then one day, without any specific reason such as a breakdown, sickness or else, I realized that I was missing out on some of the most important things in life: the enjoyment of life itself via my family, my friends, travel, the arts, etc.

From that moment onwards I changed my attitudes: although I still apply great energy towards my work, I do so during my working hours alone, shutting down completely the moment I leave my place of work, wherever that is, at home or abroad. This is something I then perfected after working in China. From the Chinese I learned to deal with each problem at a time: 'Tomorrow will take care of tomorrow.' Of course this philosophy does not work for us Westerners too well; many of our problems of life are interlocked with one another and often have to be solved together to be effective. What I did, however, was to create some bulkheads in my mind vis-a-vis personal life, professional life and social life. This allowed me at least not to mix things and to deal with each aspect of my life accordingly, and, most of all, serenely. Each bulkhead has other separations within itself so that things can be kept under control and dealt with individually.

I make a point to have physical exercise as often as possible, preferably playing tennis at least once a week in Winter and two or three times per week in Spring, Summer and Autumn. I travel a great deal and I always carry my tennis gear with me. I play with anybody, anywhere. I feel the need for the physical exercise, for the blood to flow faster and for the nervous energy to discharge. Without physical exercise and consequent relaxation to collect my thoughts I believe my mental state would suffer seriously and my judgement be impaired.

In life, I look ahead, using the past as lessons in what to do and what not to do. I will go to great lengths for the happiness and well-being of my family and for the success of my enterprises. I respect and enjoy my friends and always try not to hurt anybody if ever possible. I cherish what I have. I must not forget Religion, it plays an important part in my life in general and in times of stress in particular. I find comfort, help and reason in visiting a church and concentrating on my beliefs.

Dr Anna Maria Neuhold

Italian Medical Interpreter and Nutritionist

I come from a family where rest was synonymous with sin. It took me a good ten years of my adult life to shake this sense of guilt off whenever I felt the physical or mental need to stop.

I do not know what came first, whether I rationalized the need for relaxation or whether I gave in to relaxation before I could dissect the reason why I was doing it. I know that at some stage of my life my great passion for reading led me to learn about Skinner's Behaviourism. In a nutshell, it suggests that all our actions are either reinforced by reward or inhibited by punishment.

Both instinctively and rationally I started to feel how important it is to take small breaks even in the course of the same day. (My days are very long!)

To me relaxation now means to reward myself in a very small but consistent way. I do this at least once a day. The way I do it can vary considerably: If, after hours spent reading and writing I need to empty my mind, an energetic work-out will be the right thing: just by following my teacher's instructions I will send my brain to sleep and let my body take over. If, on the other hand, I am physically tired, sitting down with a book or one of the three-month-old articles I put aside to read, will help me recover.

I do not read fiction and my husband finds it strange that I can genuinely relax with a microbiology book or with a text on genetics. Yet I feel that the line between pleasure and relaxation is a very thin one. To me mental engagement never means physical strain and feeding my mind with subjects I enjoy seems to replenish my waning energy.

Far from being self-indulgent, relaxation, while helping myself, improves my relationship with the rest of the world: once I have recharged my batteries, I can use them to the benefit of the people I love. By acknowledging the need for and even the right to relaxation I have become a more flexible person – however, to be absolutely honest, I shall have to admit that somehow I still feel that I have to earn it, which is probably the price I have to pay for breaking one of my family's rules.

Conor Cruise O'Brien

Contributing Editor, The Atlantic, *Boston; Editor-in-Chief, the* Observer *1979–81; Pro-Chancellor, University of Dublin since 1973*

My secretary tells me that my only form of relaxation and unwinding is work! It is true that I enjoy my work – which is writing – but I find it more bracing than relaxing. For relaxation I do a lot of walking, mostly on the Hill of Howth where I live, and as this is also Gay Byrne's way of relaxing we meet on the Hill from time to time. Reading – things not connected with work – is also a form of relaxation. I read all sorts of things – history, biography, thrillers, detective stories, classics – in various quantities, depending on mood and context. I also like to relax among my friends and with members of my family, preferably over a good dinner with plenty of good wine. I don't watch television very much except for the News and The Late Late Show. But I find radio relaxing, especially on a long journey. My *Who's Who* entry lists my recreation as 'travelling' and I still find it recreational in a way and do quite a lot of it, but can't say I really find it relaxing.

Edna O'Brien

Irish Writer

It would be an exaggeration on my part to say that I relax or unwind because I don't.

I read and above all re-read great works of literature – they contain all the philosophy there is and render it through the medium of poetry. They it is that inform us about love and pain, the seven deadly sins, the world we live in and the other world that we sometimes ponder over.

In dreams begins responsibility.

EPIGRAPH FROM WILLIAM BUTLER YEATS (1865–1939)
'RESPONSIBILITIES: POEMS AND A PLAY' (1914).
ORIGINALLY AN EPIGRAPH FROM AN OLD PLAY.

Iona Opie

Folklorist

Reading provides me with relaxation, comfort, escape, and a means of bribery. I read in my bath – one of the ultimate luxuries. I read the Pooh books when I am despondent; P.G. Wodehouse when I am apprehensive; poetry when I need to revive my faith in life; and Dickens when I have to get through some tedious work – an hour's work is rewarded by ten minutes of Dickens.

I subscribe to no unified system of belief, distrusting anything, metaphysical or physical, that seems too neat and finished. My beliefs have become vaguer and vaguer and less able to be defined in words as I have grown older. I rely on old, long-accepted ideas. They are a ragbag of whatever has seemed valuable throughout my life: notions of self-discipline and honour from my childhood and from admired people like Plato and Marcus Aurelius, principles of living from the Sermon on the Mount.

God is essential to my well-being, and yet I am not sure what I mean by 'God', except that the word must be equated with goodness and the power of the spirit. When, in the aftermath of the Gulf War, an Iraqi survivor, wandering about in the desolation battlefield, said 'It is enough to make you lose your faith in God', I felt that his God and mine were the same.

I have outgrown the God of my childhood, the God who was omnipotent and to whom one applied for various benefits. Now my God is more like H.G. Wells', in *Mr Britling Sees It Through*, a God who is simply 'a very present help in time of trouble'.

Understanding grows with experience. Once I would have said that success depended on good judgement and hard work. Now I admit that luck plays a great part; it is often a matter of being in the right place at the right time. I accept, too, that misadventure is more likely to be the result of chaos than conspiracy, and that failure is more common than success.

I value the healing powers of silence, stones, and water. I enjoy the sensual pleasures of touch, taste, smell, sight, and hearing. I draw strength from the impersonality of nature and the stars. And I can best ignore the small distresses of daily life if I can keep my sense of its absurdity, constantly making fun of myself and it.

Of many favourite passages of poetry, I find myself constantly returning to this one:

Here, where the world is quiet;
  Here, where all trouble seems
Dead winds' and spent waves' riot
  In doubtful dreams of dreams;
I watch the green field growing
For reaping folk and sowing,
For harvest-time and mowing,
  A sleepy world of streams.

FROM ALGERNON CHARLES SWINBURNE (1837–1909),
'GARDEN OF PROSERPINE'

(Probably this reflects the beautiful countryside in which I live, and my own advancing age.)

The Rt. Hon. The Lord Owen of the City of Plymouth

As Dr David Owen, the Foreign Secretary 1977–79; Former Leader and Co-Founder of the SDP; Ambassador for peace in Europe

I relax and unwind best by doing any of the following: sailing, playing tennis, reading or taking a long, deep bath.

The passage from Shakespeare's *Hamlet* (Act I, Scene iii) in which Polonius advises his son Laertes, ending with the words,

> This above all: to thine own self be true,
> And it must follow, as the night the day,
> Thou canst not then be false to any man

is one which has always appealed to me as a general philosophy of life.

My favourite poem is *Candles* by C. P. Cavafy, translated by Rae Dalven. It is a reminder that so many things in life fade or die and that you must always look forward, not back:

> The days of our future stand before us
> like a row of little lighted candles –
> golden, warm, and lively little candles.

> The days gone by remain behind us,
> a mournful line of burnt-out candles,
> the nearest ones are still smoking,
> cold candles, melted and bent.

> I do not want to look at them; their form saddens me,
> and it saddens me to recall their first light.
> I look ahead at my lighted candles.

I do not want to turn back, lest I see and shudder –
how quickly the somber line lengthens,
how quickly the burnt-out candles multiply.

C. P. CAVAFY, 'CANDLES'

Sir Peter Parker, LVO

Chairman Rockware Group, PLC; Vice-Chairman Friends of the Earth Trust Ltd since 1988; Former Chairman of British Rail

My problem with relaxation is that the word is so stretchy, it covers too much sometimes, too little at others. Too much when all that I am really doing is resting, sucking a slice of orange at half-time, going blank; of course, a feet-up does ease the physical pressure, but in fact it does little to take the weight off the mind. Relaxation is too big a word, if that is all that is really happening. I certainly don't under-rate the need for the break in the game – particularly in the pell-mell life of enterprise. Among the lighthearted rules of management in my book *For Starters* I urge that one 'somehow find a way of sleeping twice a day'.

But suddenly relaxation can seem too small a word. Among those rules I suggest that you 'take your problems home'. Home can provide the sense of proportion which redeems your sense of humour. And that really is relaxation. Relaxation, in all its ambiguities, is plainly not simply taking things easy, though it does involve heart-easing things. True relaxation can be the way to concentrate on what really matters in a moment.

> To see a World in a Grain of Sand,
> And a Heaven in a Wild Flower,
> Hold Infinity in the palm of your hand,
> And Eternity in an hour.

> WILLIAM BLAKE (1757–1827), *AUGURIES OF INNOCENCE*

I once tried a course of transcendental meditation, but I was a failure at it. Stress, the guru agreed, seemed to suit me: it keeps building up, doesn't it? It keeps my act together. I value the relaxation that gives me time to re-focus willy-nilly on purposes uncomfortably broader and bigger than my own. Blake is usually to hand in my office, even in the car – but Blake is anything but cosy: 'Damn braces. Bless relaxes', he once said.

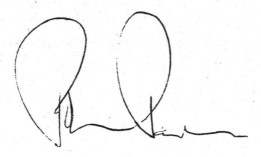

The Rt. Hon. The Lord Parry of Neyland, Dyfed

Chairman, Clean World International

Relaxing and unwinding has never been for me a problem – sometimes finding the space in which to relax and unwind is. Many busy people believe in their hearts that they are lazy, and drive themselves forward in order to compensate. Secretly, I see myself as one of those.

Having been brought up in a Welsh family, having lived almost constantly within the family of Wales, being influenced by my father's work and personality as a pastor of a Welsh congregation, I have happily surrounded myself with people. I love the group crowd occasions, whether they be huge public meetings or smaller, family occasions. If I had been asked some years ago, I would have said that I disliked being alone. All that has altered as I have grown older. Above all things these days, I cherish space to be alone. It is what I call 'looking at the wall'. My current lifestyle occasionally gives me that space. I sit in a small apartment in London during the dying hours of the day, and do nothing other than relax and unwind. For an hour or two I am responsible for, and to, nothing and nobody. I am alone without being lonely.

There are other things which I do which are a total therapy: writing and reading, singing – badly and off-key, but happily – and generally being a Welshman in a wide world of travel. The great bonus of my life has been the privilege of travelling the world, which has come to me almost accidentally because of the other things which I have done.

Having been conditioned as a fairly conventional, fundamentalist Christian, I now see myself as a believer in the central thesis, rather than in the fundamental detail of Christian teaching. When they asked Christ what was the most important commandment in the law, he said 'This is my commandment, that ye love one another.' I believe that love is a physical force. There have been moments of trauma in my life – for example, after suffering multiple injuries in a motor accident – when I have actually been sustained by the evidence of love around me. Letters which I received from total strangers were as important to me then as the obvious concern of those who shared my life. For me, then, God is Love.

As I recovered consciousness from the first of the series of major operations that followed, I was singing the words of a hymn from my childhood. The words were taken up from neighbouring beds in the hospital wards. During the several months of recovery which followed, the morning singing of the words became a ritual.

> When upon life's billows, you are tempest tossed,
> When you are discouraged, thinking all is lost,
> Count your many blessings, name them one by one,
> And it will surprise you, what the Lord has done.

Gordon Ramey.

Nicholas Parsons

Actor; Presenter; Director

I suppose my main form of relaxation is to fall asleep for short periods whenever possible. Because of my very busy professional life and heavy charitable commitments, I find that taking a catnap is an immediate way to rebuild my energy, and restore my physical and mental wellbeing. Immediately, I can move on to the next stage of the day with renewed vigour.

I also find activities such as gardening, sport and games generally very relaxing. The physical activity involved in gardening, as well as its creative aspects, help me to unwind from the pressure built up from intense mental activity. For as long as I can remember sport has been a major part of my life, and the concentration of the mind and body when playing cricket or golf is also a wonderful way to release the built-up pressures and stresses of life today.

In short, my recipe for a relaxing day would be as follows:

Some sporting activity; a leisurely meal; then an afternoon sleep; a little gardening, followed by a quiet evening reading or perhaps watching television.

The chances of achieving this in my very busy life are few and far between – but I try!

The second question is more difficult to answer as my philosophy of life has changed with the passing years. Also, it would take much more than a short paragraph for me to answer this.

I find it very easy to like people, and become very distressed by the amount of hatred, cruelty and violence in the world. We are all different, thank goodness. If loving someone is difficult, it is so easy to accept them. There is too much stress in most people's lives, and there is a great deal of envy. So much in our society today feeds on envy, the most negative of emotions, which in turn can lead to hatred and violence. Envy suppresses individual spirit; love releases it. It is significant that the negative traits I have mentioned disappear in time of war and disaster, which seem to bring out the best in people, when they are faced by a common enemy or human tragedy. What a sadness that in times of peace and plenty the same emotions cannot govern actions.

I have always been impressed by the writings of Kahlil Gibran, the Eastern poet, philosopher and artist, who was born near Mount Lebanon. He has the wonderful ability to express so much of life's hidden depths. As someone who loves children, his poem about children is most moving, and even inspirational.

> Your children are not your children.
> They are the sons and daughters of Life's
> longing for itself.
> They come through you but not from you,
> And though they are with you yet they belong
> not to you.

'CHILDREN', FIRST VERSE FROM *THE PROPHET*
BY KAHLIL GIBRAN (1883–1931)

Nicholas Parsons

Jonathon Porritt

*Environmentalist; Director, Friends of the Earth 1984–90;
Freelance Writer; Broadcaster*

In order to be at home in the world, we must be *fully* of it, experience it *directly* as mud between our toes, as the rough bark on a tree, as the song of the world awakening every morning. The Earth speaks to something in every person, even when we are imprisoned by concrete and steel. In that dialogue lies a form of celebration as primitively powerful as anything to be found in our anaemic, emaciated culture.

Beyond that, *learning* how to celebrate is a very personal thing. For me, it has always been through trees, both through the direct personal experience of trees and through the writing of others who share the same kind of feeling. My childhood was spent on Hampstead Heath, a small patch of semi-natural green in the middle of London. It is small in real terms, no more than a couple of hundred acres. But through the eyes of an eight-year-old boy, it was absolutely huge; indeed, much too large to be properly encompassed at ground level. So my first relationship with trees started predictably: God had obviously put them on Earth for me to climb, and, given my immersion in a comprehensively competitive culture, it wasn't enough first to climb trees; I had to climb the very *highest* trees. I first learned about nature and my interdependence with nature, hanging precariously out of the branches of these wonderful, long-suffering trees, taking equal pleasure in the sense of danger, the sense of isolation and the sense of being utterly at home. My mother's apprehension that I was actually *regressing* in evolutionary terms (after all, our primate ancestors had come *down* out of the trees, so who was I to reverse this earth-shattering trend?) made little impact. From that time on I was completely hooked and I remain an unreconstructed dendrophile to this day, which is why

President Reagan's comment, 'Seen one tree, seen 'em all' doesn't really strike home with me!

Since then I've encountered many trees, many woods, many forests, and fashioned many intimate relations with those trees. I've found myself replenished, enriched, enthused (in the literal sense of the word) in more ways than I could begin to describe. Through this I have become part of a spiritual community that embraces people of every culture, every country, every creed.

Marguerite Porter

Guest Artist, Royal Ballet Company since 1986
(Senior Principal Dancer, 1976–1985)

A dancer's life has be one of the most stressful lives possible. Having recently left the Royal Ballet Company, of which I was a member for over twenty years, I realize (rather late) that during those stress-filled, and highly pressurized years I never relaxed, either mentally or physically!

I could never really relax my body, not even during holidays, because there was always the worry of getting oneself back into peak condition. It was therefore easier to keep the engine running all the time.

I found the mental strain of a ballerina's life enormous also and never really learnt to deal with the nerves.

Looking back now, I wonder quite how I survived it all. I think my sense of humour usually saved the day, along with my own very personal faith in God.

My life could not be more different now – wife, mother and teacher. Although, of course, there are still stressful and exhausting times, nothing compares with that of my life as a ballerina. I find aromatherapy and reflexology very soothing and helpful. I make time for that at least once a month. Most of all, however, I feel the greatest antidote to stress is fulfilment and happiness and I am very blessed that, in my family, I have found both.

Dame Shirley Porter, DBE, DL

Former Lord Mayor of Westminster; Chairman of LBC

There are three main ways in which I combat stress. I practise meditation, which involves deep concentration on a single word for a period of twenty minutes. I also practise yoga and take part in vigorous exercise including power walking, tennis, swimming and golf.

Syed A. Rafique

Barrister/Solicitor/Journalist (retd.); Advocate Supreme Court of Pakistan

I am now 87 years of age and generally speaking in perfect health, except for my eyes and even they do not present any difficulty except for reading. This eye problem dates from my childhood when my eyes were so bad that I had to give up my studies for a couple of years.

I attribute the reason for my good health to yoga exercises which I started doing when I came to this country in 1921. The most effective exercise is relaxation.

This is quite simple. You think of your fingers or toes and realize that they are taut and you release that tautness by conscious effort. Do the same with elbows, neck, legs and feet till you feel that you are dead. In fact each relaxation means being consciously dead, not by divine rule, but by your own effort.

The poem that always comes to my mind while doing this is the quatrain by Wordsworth about the dancing daffodils.

> I wandered lonely as a cloud
> That floats on high o'er vales and hills,
> When all at once I saw a crowd,
> A host, of golden daffodils . . .
>
> WILLIAM WORDSWORTH (1770–1850), *I WANDERED LONELY AS A CLOUD*

I hope that my few words will enable people to get more out of life and be more tolerant and helpful to each other.

Kathleen Raine, D.Litt., D.Litt., D.Litt.

Poet; Blake Scholar; Editor, Temenos, a Review devoted to the Arts of the Imagination; Awarded the Queen's Gold Medal for Poetry in December 1992

Although I am most irregular and inattentive in any attempt at formal meditation, I do every (or nearly every) evening light a candle and a stick of incense and give my mind to reflection on invisible things. Otherwise, I commune with my garden. To me nature is a daily epiphany.

My philosophy of life? For half a lifetime I have been a scholar of the perennial wisdom, first in Blake, then the Neoplatonists, then Yeats, Blake's greatest disciple and first editor, and thence to India. I no longer look to any religion as a commitment, but have learned deeply from all, but reality is beyond all formulations or expressions. That reality is a living mystery, unknowable but endlessly producing marvels from its inexhaustible treasuries. A spiritual Presence, 'a motion and a spirit that moves through all things'. In this sense, a Person.

> I've read all the books but one
> Only remains sacred: this
> Volume of wonders, open
> Always before my eyes.

Irina Ratushinskaya

Russian Poet and Writer

I WILL LIVE AND SURVIVE

I will live and survive and be asked:
How they slammed my head against a trestle,
How I had to freeze at nights,
How my hair started to turn grey . . .
But I'll smile. And will crack some joke
And brush away the encroaching shadow.
And I will render homage to the dry September
That became my second birth.
And I'll be asked: 'Doesn't it hurt you to remember?'
Not being deceived by my outward flippancy.
But the former names will detonate in my memory –
Magnificent as old cannon.
And I will tell of the best people in all the earth,
The most tender, but also the most invincible,
How they said farewell, how they went to be tortured,
How they waited for letters from their loved ones.
And I'll be asked: what helped us to live
When there were neither letters nor any news – only walls,
And the cold of the cell, and the blather of official lies,
And the sickening promises made in exchange for betrayal.
And I will tell of the first beauty
I saw in captivity.
A frost-covered window! No spyholes, nor walls,
Nor cell-bars, nor the long-endured pain –
Only a blue radiance on a tiny pane of glass,

A cast pattern – none more beautiful could be dreamt!
The more clearly you looked, the more powerfully blossomed
Those brigand forests, campfires and birds!
And how many times there was bitter cold weather
And how many windows sparkled after that one –
But never was it repeated,
That upheaval of rainbow ice!
And anyway, what good would it be to me now,
And what would be the pretext for that festival?
Such a gift can only be received once,
And perhaps is only needed once.

FROM 'NO I'M NOT AFRAID' (30 NOVEMBER 1983)

Author's note: This poem was written by Irina Ratushinskaya while in prison in November 1983. In March 1983 Irina was sentenced to seven years' hard labour and five years' internal exile, accused of anti-Soviet agitation and propaganda. Her crime: writing poetry. She was released from prison in Kiev in October 1986. She agreed with me that her philosophy of life shines forth from this poem like a lit beacon and has permitted me to include it in *The Relaxation Letters*.

Claire Rayner

Writer and Broadcaster

You ask me how I cope with stress. I find the best way is to make sure my relationships are in good health – it's my husband and grown-up children and young daughters-in-law who keep my feet very much on the ground – and also I get a lot of exercise. The more tired I am, the more hectic things get, the more important it is that I fit a half-mile swim into the day.

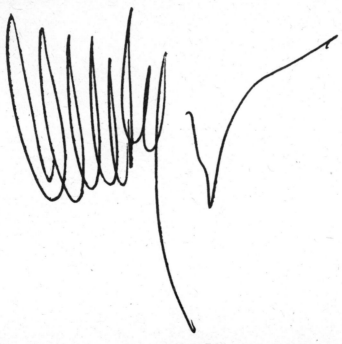

Beryl Reid, OBE

Actress

I relax and unwind by being in my own home and watching the cats do something similar.

My general philosophy of life is live it, and if you are lucky enough to know when you are happy (*at the time*) you are a winner.

Beryl Reid

Trewin Restorick

Director of the environmental organization Global Action Plan

The poem or passage which has most inspired me is by Joe Miller, an artist who lives in the State of Washington, USA:

> If the Earth were only a few feet in diameter, floating a few feet above a field somewhere, people would come from everywhere to marvel at it. People would walk around it marvelling at its big pools of water, its little pools and the water flowing between. People would marvel at the bumps on it and the holes in it. They would marvel at the very thin layer of gas surrounding it and the water suspended in the gas. The people would marvel at all the creatures walking around the surface of the ball and at the creatures in the water. The people would declare it as sacred because it was the only one, and they would protect it so that it would not be hurt. The ball would be the greatest wonder known, and people would come to pray to it, to be healed, to gain knowledge, to know beauty and to wonder how it could be. People would love it and defend it with their lives because they would somehow know that their lives could be nothing without it. If the Earth were only a few feet in diameter.

Having thought about how I relax, I came to the rather bizarre conclusion that it is by standing on a football terrace on a cold winter's night watching 22 men trying, usually unsuccessfully, to play football. I guess there is no accounting for taste!

Dr Jonathan Rhoads, MD

Hospital of the University of Pennsylvania, USA

Contrary to prevailing views, I have looked upon stress as something to seek rather than to avoid or recover from. Admittedly, one does not want to have it continuously or for too long a period at a time and I have been fortunate in this regard. My career has been in general surgery. There have, of course, been many tense moments both in the operating room and in deciding who should undergo an operation or have another treatment recommended. One habit which I formed early when confronted with a difficult decision was to posit that things would turn out as badly as possible and to ask myself in advance what course of action I would feel best satisfied with if, in point of fact, things did go that badly. This not only led me to be more thorough and more cautious but avoided regrets that I had not taken additional precautions in managing the case.

One is confronted in surgery not infrequently with alternative courses of action between which a choice must be made because 'no action' promises such a bad result. If one chooses action 'A' and the patient does well, one feels a glow of satisfaction. However, if one chooses action 'A' and the patient does badly, one always wonders whether the patient might have done better had one taken action 'B'. Usually, one never knows that it would have made any difference but the doubt lingers.

Long ago I admitted to myself that I could not always be right and that I had to expect not only a number of failures that were inevitable but some failures that perhaps were my fault, and I made up my mind to live with this and to do the best I could, always trying to do for others as I would have them do for me under the circumstances.

In the eulogy of Dr Samuel David Gross, Professor of Surgery at

Jefferson Medical College in Philadelphia and founder of the American Surgical Association, S. Weir Mitchell wrote: 'Work was his only play – strange paradox. He rejoiced in this use of himself. To be long away from work wearied him so that there went to the perfecting of his everyday business, duty and the pleasure which others get out of holidays.' In a lesser way I, too, found my enjoyment in my work and did not develop athletic or cultural avocations to any extent. However, beginning in middle years, after a bout with tuberculosis, I regularly took a month away during the summer usually spending it with my wife and various groups of our six children climbing mountains and doing carpentry or other building at a summer vacation home in the White Mountains of New Hampshire.

There was a large motto which hung in my parents' dining room which was carefully lettered by an elderly patient of my father's who was unable to pay for services. It read 'Hitherto hath the Lord helped us.' Whether one attributes one's good fortune to the Deity or to factors of chance, I have indeed been very fortunate. Certainly, there are many others who have accomplished much more but I do not envy them and perhaps this, also, frees one from excessive stress as the compulsion to surpass others is often doomed to failure and disappointment.

Jonathan Rhoads

Angela Rippon

Journalist; Radio and Television Presenter

Generally I relax and unwind by listening to music, going to the theatre, reading and working on *petit point*. Also, when I have the opportunity I love to ride my own horse down in Devon.

I suppose my general philosophy of life is trying not to be negative, only to be positive, and not wasting time and effort on things in the past that I cannot change, and looking forward to the future over which I may have some influence.

I would not say that this has necessarily been a quotation that has in any way affected my life, but I did feel it to be a particularly wise piece of work that contains a truth which might be worth following:

If of thy worldly goods thou art bereft
And in thy slender store two loaves alone to thee are left,
Sell one
And with the boon buy hyacinths to feed the soul.

I am told it is a translation of an old Persian prophet. I believe there is wisdom in it, for it speaks volumes about not always seeking material things, but occasionally taking time out, as we might say here in Britain, 'to smell the roses'.

Anita Roddick, OBE

Founder, The Body Shop Int. PLC

The thought that every day might be my last, and the desire to make the most of every moment, drives me on.

I have always said that I would rather wear out than rust to death and, thank God, I still seem to have as much energy now as when I started the first shop in 1976. I think the older you get the more you realize that this is no dress rehearsal, so you feel you want to put more into life. I am always astonished and grateful, when I wake up in the morning, to be alive. The thought that every day might be my last, and the desire to make the most of every moment, drives me on.

Ever since I was a small girl I have always had an abhorrence of death. I am not of the Buddhist school of thought which says that death is a passage to another life. I want to know what is happening in this world, not the next. Balancing a fear of death with living life as if you have only got one day left certainly concentrates the mind.

EXTRACT FROM *BODY AND SOUL*, BY ANITA RODDICK

The Rt. Hon. Dame Angela Rumbold, DBE, CBE, MP

Deputy Chairman of the Conservative Party

You ask how I relax and unwind and I can say, I think with complete truth, that there are two ways in which I totally relax: one is to curl up with a good novel, preferably one that I know I am going to enjoy, and the other is to go for a swim. Whilst I am swimming up and down a pool I find myself completely relaxed and able to cast aside any stress or worries that I have. Therefore the absolutely ideal situation for me to be able to relax totally is to first of all have a swim and secondly to follow it up with a good book.

You also asked about my general philosophy of life, which I think has developed over the years. Nowadays I am very much a person who takes each day as it comes, recognizing that some will be more stressful than others, and that on occasions every single thing that one attempts to do somehow or another contrives to go wrong. I believe that life is full of checks and balances and that for every bad thing that happens there will always be something to balance it that will be good; in this way I really do manage to keep myself at least relatively fit in mind, if not in body!

My favourite piece of poetry is from Alexander Pope:

All nature is but art unknown to thee,
All chance, direction which thou canst not see;
All discord, harmony not understood;
All partial evil, universal good;
And, spite of pride, in erring reason's spite,
One truth is clear, Whatever is, is right.

ALEXANDER POPE (1688–1744), *AN ESSAY ON MAN*

Anthony Russell-Roberts

Administrative Director of The Royal Ballet, Covent Garden

As soon as I come home from work I try to relax. I picture two imaginary taps on either side of my head by each temple which I make a conscious decision to turn off. It is almost a physical sensation when I do this, and I find it most comforting. If the phone rings about work I deliberately turn the taps on again before dealing with the problem.

I like to relax by listening to classical music or opera, lying comfortably on a sofa with my feet up, propped up by large cushions. At bedtime I listen to a carefully chosen piece of music through headphones, secure in the knowledge that the machine can switch itself off at the end, so I don't have to worry about falling asleep.

Weekends in the country are also a great relaxation. I enjoy gentle gardening, such as tying up and deadheading roses and going for long, slow walks in remote countryside, seeing as few houses and people as possible. When the weather is good, I like lounging around on a chaise longue in a favourite part of the garden, reading idly with every intention of nodding off.

Lady Ryder of Warsaw, CMG, OBE

Founder and Social Worker, Sue Ryder Foundation for the Sick and Disabled of All Age Groups in Great Britain and Overseas

Prayer enables me to direct my life and periodically throughout the day I make use of the chapel here at Headquarters to gain perspective, which centres upon the daily Mass. I say also very early morning and night prayers.

My philosophy of life: to follow the philosophy of the Foundation which bears my name to serve the sick and handicapped of all age groups both in Britain and overseas.

The following is part of a longer prayer/poem by Frank J. Exley which I quote in my autobiography *Child of my Love:*

Child of my love, fear not the unknown morrow
Dread not the new demand life makes of thee
Thy ignorance doth hold no cause for sorrow
For what thou knowest not is known.

Ryder of Warsaw

Dr Steven B. Sample

President, and Professor of Electrical Engineering, University of Southern California

The most relaxing thing I do is spend twenty minutes each day reading books that are as far removed as possible from my two professions of electrical engineering and university administration. In this way I go through about a dozen books a year, which taken together over several years form a wonderful eclectic assortment that encompasses history, philosophy, biography, the sciences, poetry, and fiction (which last must be at least fifty years old, and of good reputation, since it's so difficult to separate the wheat from the chaff in modern fiction). Recent new members of this assortment include Plato's *Republic*, Einstein's *Relativity*, Dante's *Divine Comedy*, Joseph Conrad's *Heart of Darkness*, Darwin's *Origin of Species*, Bruce Lancaster's history of *The American Revolution*, the autobiographical *Education of Henry Adams*, Jane Austen's *Pride and Prejudice*, and Sophocles' *Oedipus the King*. As it turns out, liberal education is much more meaningful and fun when one is over forty!

My *philosophy* of life, as opposed to the way I actually *live* my life, is based essentially on the Christian gospels. I agree with the apostle Paul that everything in this world is ephemeral and of no permanent value save for an act of unselfish kindness toward another human being. In actual fact I pursue the vanities of this world with much the same gusto as my fellow men, but deep down I believe that, here on earth, only love and charity have any real meaning in the long run.

The single passage of literature to which I turn most often for inspiration was written nearly four centuries ago by the English lawyer and poet John Donne:

No man is an island, entire of itself; every man is a piece of the continent, a part of the main; if a clod be washed away by the sea, Europe is the less, as well as if a promontory were, as well as if a manor of thy friends or of thine own were; any man's death diminishes me, because I am involved in Mankind; And therefore never send to know for whom the bell tolls; It tolls for thee.

JOHN DONNE (1571?–1631), *DEVOTIONS*

Charles Secrett

Executive Director of Friends of the Earth

I unwind by dreaming and taking exercise – mostly swimming and saunas. I relax when I am with my family.

My general philosophy of life is 'live and let live'.

These lines have inspired me:

In Xanadu did Kubla Khan
A stately pleasure-dome decree:
Where Alph, the sacred river, ran
Through caverns measureless to man
  Down to a sunless sea.
So twice five miles of fertile ground
With walls and towers were girdled round:
And there were gardens bright with sinuous rills,
Where blossomed many an incense-bearing tree;
And here were forests ancient as the hills,
Enfolding sunny spots of greenery.
SAMUEL TAYLOR COLERIDGE (1772–1834), *KUBLA KHAN*

Dennis Selinger

Theatrical Agent

I relax and unwind by playing cards with my friends – none of whom are in my business.

My general philosophy of life is to try anything once as long as it doesn't hurt anyone. If you enjoy it, keep doing it – but in moderation! Above all, never lose your sense of humour.

A quote that has inspired me: I don't know who originally said it, but 'Do unto others as you would do unto yourself.'

Peter Shilton, MBE

British Footballer; Team Manager

How do I relax and unwind: watching TV, walking the dogs, golf and horse racing.

My philosophy of life is to take each day at a time and do your best.

A quotation that has inspired me:

You only get out of something what you put in.

Antoinette Sibley, CBE

Former Prima Ballerina, The Royal Ballet, Covent Garden;
President, The Royal Academy of Dancing

TO UNWIND

When everything gets 'on top' of me. I try to snatch half an hour in the afternoon to lie on my bed with phones *off* and no-one to disturb me. If I'm in my car I listen to Beethoven's Moonlight Sonata, Pathétique or Appassionata piano sonatas, or Harry Belafonte.

If I'm in the country I go for long walks. Even in London before a difficult performance I would get to the Royal Opera House early and walk around what was the Market.

I'll just lie Zombie-like watching almost anything on TV.

TO RELAX

In the country – I like to go on my bike with the wind flying through my hair.

I listen to any music by Mozart. Arias from Verdi's Masked Ball, Traviata, Aida; Puccini's La Bohème, Turandot and, of course, Mozart's Marriage of Figaro.

In the evenings I like to go to the Opera or eat out at restaurants with my friends or family.

Most unusual but a great treat (only have time in the holidays) is to sit in the hot summer sun under a parasol reading a book.

PHILOSOPHY

I've never really thought about a general philosophy of life. I suppose it is to do the best we can.

WORDS THAT HAVE INSPIRED ME

Nil Desparendum was my father's motto. He wrote it down for me and I always carry it around in my wallet.

A wise man once said to me (a born worrier) – '*Never* worry about things you can do nothing about. Only worry about things you can do *something* about.'

My own maxim has always been – 'Where there's a will there's a way.'

These have all helped me no end.

Robert Smith

Director, UNICEF UK

As a lover of the theatre, and above all of Shakespeare, I suppose I turn to our greatest poet and playwright more than to any other source for wisdom and inspiration.

Prospero's words have strength and nobility in resignation, the power to move, to purify, to humble human pride yet uplift the spirit.

> Our revels now are ended. These our actors,
> As I foretold you, were all spirits and
> Are melted into air, into thin air:
> And, like the baseless fabric of this vision,
> The cloud-capp'd towers, the gorgeous palaces,
> The solemn temples, the great globe itself,
> Yea, all which it inherit, shall dissolve
> And, like this insubstantial pageant faded,
> Leave not a rack behind. We are such stuff
> As dreams are made on, and our little life
> Is rounded with a sleep.

WILLIAM SHAKESPEARE (1564–1616), *THE TEMPEST,* ACT IV, SCENE i

Sir Georg Solti, KBE

Music Director, Chicago Symphony Orchestra, 1969–Sept. 1991, Music Director Laureate from Sept. 1991; Principal Conductor and Artistic Director, London Philharmonic Orchestra, 1979–83, then Conductor Emeritus

My chief relaxations are playing tennis, bridge, reading and bicycle-riding.

My general philosophy of life includes the importance of hard work and to strive to be better at whatever one does.

Tommy Steele, OBE

Singer, Actor, Entertainer

I relax by reading.
My philosophy of life is to always be optimistic, in spite of adversity.
The poem which gives me inspiration in my life is 'If' by Rudyard Kipling.

> If you can talk with crowds and keep your virtue,
>   Or walk with Kings – nor lose the common touch,
> If neither foes nor loving friends can hurt you,
>   If all men count with you, but none too much;
>
> If you can fill the unforgiving minute
>   With sixty seconds' worth of distance run,
> Yours is the Earth and everything that's in it,
>   And – which is more – you'll be a Man, my son!

RUDYARD KIPLING (1865–1936), 'IF', LAST TWO VERSES

Jackie Stewart, OBE

Ex-Grand Prix World Motor Racing Champion; Businessman

Stress has been a major part of my life for almost as long as I can remember. At school it was because of dyslexia. Immediately after school I wanted to work hard in my father's garage to prove myself. Then came the stress of competitive clay-pigeon shooting, in which I became reasonably successful, followed immediately by motor-sport which has since given way to a very hectic business life.

I feel stress is what you make of it. What would be horribly stressful for some is completely manageable for others. You learn how to deal with it through paying great attention to the messages your body gives you.

What I have found to be absolutely essential is to have a good amount of sleep, avoid alcohol as much as possible, eat sensibly, and not take oneself too seriously! There is nothing wrong with being conscientious, but there is no point in being constipated in life by not being able to have a good laugh at yourself and meet with amusing friends.

My father frequently told me 'see yourself as others see you' as well as 'you can kid a lot of people but you can't fool yourself'! A good laugh I think is probably the best therapy of all. I find reading light novels an 'escape' and exercise and physical fitness an amazing mental therapy, which of course also requires discipline.

Dr Elisabeth D. Svendsen, MBE, DVMS

Founded The Donkey Sanctuary, Sidmouth, Devon, England in 1969, which has now grown into nine farms and has taken into care over 5700 donkeys. Also runs The Slade Centre, an indoor riding centre for handicapped children, The International Donkey Protection Trust to improve conditions for donkeys throughout the world, and her own Trust for Children and Donkeys, whose aim is to provide riding units for disabled children throughout the country

My general philosophy on life – I always live each day as if it were the last and I have always had a great love of both people and animals, particularly those in trouble. I get most pleasure from helping those in need and fortunately my travels have allowed me to offer a lifeline to people in countries as far away as Ethiopia, Kenya and Mexico. My main love, however, is for animals: I feel every creature has a right to as good a life as possible and I do my best to reverse cruelties and indignations inflicted on all animals and, in particular, the humble donkey.

How to relax and unwind – I have a large garden which I have turned into an aviary and I relax sitting in there watching 200 of my rescued birds living a life of relative freedom. I also love antiques and collect various small objects of antiquity and history which gives me pleasure.

During times of stress, facing practical or emotional problems, a poem I was read in school has always inspired me:

He that is down needs fear no fall
He that is low no pride
He that is humble ever shall
Have God to be his guide.

Mother Teresa, MC, Hon. OM, Hon. OBE

Albanian-born Roman Catholic Missionary

LOVE TO PRAY

feel often during the day the need for prayer
and take trouble to pray.
Prayer enlarges the heart until it is capable of
containing God's gift of Himself.
Ask and seek, and your heart will grow big enough
to receive Him and keep Him as your own.

Mary, Mother of Jesus, give me your heart,
so beautiful, so pure, so Immaculate, so full of love
and humility that I may be able to receive Jesus
in the Bread of Life, love Him as you loved Him and
serve Him in the distressing disguise of the
Poorest of the Poor.

AMEN

Author's note: Mother Teresa provided me with these two prayers for inclusion in the book.

Richard Todd, OBE

Actor

I relax and unwind with a glass of whiskey and a crossword puzzle.

My philosophy of life comes from the motto stencilled on the wardrobe of my childhood bedroom and never forgotten: 'Pleasure is due when duty is done.'

A quotation from my mother's entry in my first autograph book:

Many people set out to leave their footprints in the sands of time and finish up leaving their fingerprints at Scotland Yard!

Richard Todd.

Chaim Topol

Actor/Director

I cannot speak generally on ways to help in these stress-laden times. However, what I usually do after a show when I want to unwind is go home and draw for a couple of hours. I normally draw portraits or scenes involving people. I find this most relaxing and enjoyable.

Bill Travers

Actor; Trustee, the Born Free Foundation

The trouble is, the moment I have convinced myself I am relaxed then I feel a surge of anxiety wondering how long it will last, and have I the time. If I do manage to unwind eventually I realize I am floating, barely conscious, like a hot air balloon – hollow – aimlessly towards the power lines. The awful realization triggers the burn so now I don't bother.

Whenever I feel the urge to relax and unwind I think of all those beautiful wild animals and their babies with which we share this world, miserably rotting in their horrible stinking little prisons, and the people who keep them there in utter deprivation – so our human children can have a fun day at the zoo. And I'm on my feet in a flash. Completely re-wound.

One day the spring will break I tell myself – then will be soon enough . . . .

Ah – philosophy – if only we didn't have to use words. We've swamped each other and drowned our thoughts with too many words.

A quotation that has inspired me:

Horas non numero nisi serenas. (I count only the golden hours.)

Dorothy Tutin, CBE

Actress (Stage and Films)

The following are a few statements I find interesting, helpful and sometimes inspiring:

The Artistic Temperament is a disease that afflicts Amateurs.

G.K. CHESTERTON

Your talent will select what is useful to itself. If you are attentive and concentrate you learn so much from what is wrong.

The audience has made a sincere act of HOPE!

A man is most alive when his security is taken away from him.

Fear knocked on the door. Faith answered it, and there was no one there.

When the light from above touches the mind, it tickles the mind, and it is the tickling of the mind which produces humour.

The Most Reverend Desmond M. Tutu, DD, FKC

The Anglican Archbishop of Cape Town

I would agree that relaxation is vitally important to our spiritual and physical well-being. I take a brisk walk every morning, usually about 6.00 a.m., it is an important part of my regimen. But for real relaxation there is nothing like lying on my back on the floor and letting the music of Beethoven wash over me.

My philosophy of life is that all people are created in the image of God and are therefore of infinite worth. We are bound together as brothers and sisters and we should care about each and every person as we do for our blood brothers and sisters. We should care whether they are hungry, or naked, uneducated, or ill-housed. When we care about these things we will seek for justice. It is only through justice that peace is a possibility and it is only through other people we can discover our own humanity.

Some words that have inspired me are from Romans, 5: 8:

God shows his love for us in that while we were yet sinners Christ died for us.

Dame Ninette de Valois, CH, DBE, CBE

Founder and Director of The Royal Ballet 1931–63; Founder of The Royal Ballet School (formerly The Sadler's Wells School of Ballet)

In the world of ballet a good teacher is always telling her pupils to 'relax'. She means by this to avoid tension of the muscles, which is dangerous and can lead to overstrain and accidents. Hence the importance of understanding the meaning of relaxation in relation to the execution of ballet. It does help anyone who has studied ballet to relax automatically, even in movements that do not bear any relation to the execution of ballet.

Ninette de Valois

Rev. Dr Chad Varah, OBE

Founder of the Samaritans

My philosophy of life is based on my own understanding of the Christian faith as taught by the best minds in the Church of England over the centuries. Some insights also came from the late Dr Rudolf Steiner.

We are placed here on earth to learn how to love. Everything we do and experience is making us more loving or less loving human beings. Naturally, in order to love God and our neighbour as ourselves, we need to stay alive, so that there are all sorts of things we need to learn for self-preservation. I founded The Samaritans to save the lives of as many people as possible who were likely to commit suicide. I have consistently opposed those who have tried to climb on to our bandwagon in order to pervert this humanitarian exercise into an evangelistic one. Saving lives is obviously more important than 'saving souls' which, if it can be done at all, can't be done if the person is dead.

As a Christian priest, I administer the Sacraments to those who want them, and I present to those who will listen my account of a reasonable faith, which will either strike a chord in the listener, or will not. That is up to him or her. If anything I teach helps people to be more loving to one another, I am glad. I myself do not believe that I can love as I was meant to do without loving God and receiving from Him, Whose Name and Nature is Love, the power to love the other person in a non-possessive, non-oppressive way.

Christians believe not only in the immortality of the soul, but in the resurrection of the body. I cannot interpret this in any other way than reincarnation. I believe that we all live many times on earth in our progress towards the time when we shall no longer need earthly incarnation. I do not remember any previous incarnations of my own, but I do know that I was born knowing how to read.

You ask how I 'relax and unwind'. I don't. I follow the advice, 'whatsoever thou doest, do it with thy might' – my mind is busy all my waking hours, either with my work or with my recreations: reading, listening to music, watching wild life programmes on video. When I am tired, I go to bed and flop, letting all my limbs feel heavy and letting my mind rest. I quickly fall asleep and on waking thank God that I mostly sleep like a log and mostly don't hurt anywhere. At the time of writing I am 81, and I expect to live a good many more years because there are so many things I want to do. One which should concern UNICEF is the abolition of the genital mutilation of little girls.

To be nobody but yourself in a world which is doing its best night and day to make you everybody else, is to fight the hardest battle which any human being can fight, and never stop fighting.

E. E. CUMMINGS (1894–1962)

Joni Van Der Veen

American Professional Triathlete, World and National Age Group Champion

In January of 1972, I was a divorced mother of a three-year-old son, Bryan, working as a medical technician in the local hospital and waitressing at night to make ends meet. While skiing with friends in Vermont, I encountered a nasty patch of ice, lost control and literally skied off the edge of the mountain; I fell about one hundred feet down into a ravine. Bloody and broken, I slipped into that wonderful world of light, peace, and tranquillity where only love exists. But thoughts of my son being left behind made me turn from the light and open my eyes. The peace was gone, only hot pain existed. The ski patrolmen kept me alive until the journey to a small Vermont hospital was completed. There the doctors found I had fractured my skull, collapsed both lungs, fractured seventeen vertebrae in my neck and back, four inches of the thoracic spine being completely crushed. I have only two memories. One, hearing someone say, 'Go call her parents. She won't survive the night.' And two, feeling my unquestioning faith in God, knowing His love was within me and He would not let go of me. God was holding me so I could go on holding my son, Bryan.

Recovery was long and uncertain. Eight months after the fall I underwent a nine-hour operation in New York City so my spine could be stabilized and regain the ability to walk. I was put in a full body plaster cast for the next eleven months. Wrapped in the cast, I felt fine. I was safe. I never hurt. When they cut it off, I lost my security blanket. My back hurt so much and I did not walk well. There was permanent nerve damage to my right side, and I was two inches shorter. My self-esteem and confidence could fit in a thimble. The doctors said I had to begin swimming to strengthen my back. This terrified me as I had never learned to swim as a child, but my son, who was now five, was on a swimming team winning medals. He became my coach and in a very short time, we were swimming side-by-side. In a few months, I began to look better, stand straighter, and feel stronger. Slowly a challenge emerged. Could I build back the strong confident body I lost on the side of that mountain? It would take more than swimming. I bought a pair of jogging shoes, opened my front door, and attempted to jog around the block. What a sight I must have made as I struggled to run, but in time the jogging became running and the more I did, the better I felt. I started entering road races and after a year I entered my first marathon, New York City. I paid no attention to how fast I was running, but in all the races I would cross the finish line always in the top five female finishers. This gave me a very personal sense of accomplishment, especially since I was forty years old.

Since 1985, I have been competing in the sport of triathlon, which is a race where you swim, bike, and run. I have competed in over 100 triathlons, five of them being the Ironman. This race is a 2.4 mile ocean swim, followed by a 112 mile bike race, followed by a 26.2 mile marathon run. I have had the great fortune of winning my age group in three of these and finishing third in two. But more rewarding than winning is that training and competing in these races has given me the strong healthy body I had lost.

I hope you understand why I go out my front door everyday and run, and why I don't care what anyone thinks of my passion for keeping my body healthy and at its best. The accident not only altered my perspective, it taught me to take nothing for granted and to appreciate each day. In conjunction with my recuperation, I learned respect for the human body, respect for others, and most importantly, respect for myself. I no longer define myself in relation to other people. The hours I spend alone training have made me very independent. I am challenged now to share what all this has taught me. If people know what I went through, maybe they could apply it to their own situations and say,

'If she can do it, so can I.'

My sharing has taken a more concrete form in the past two years. I began working as a personal fitness trainer for women over forty. I develop an individual daily exercise program for my clients that they aim to keep for the rest of their lives. I love seeing the gift of confidence and self-esteem that comes from exercise.

How do I see life? My two favourite quotations will give you the answer. From the *Confessions of Saint Augustine*, the last sentence of chapter six: 'Run and I will hold you and I will bring you through and there also I will hold you.'

To go forward in life we must all open doors, as you will never know until you try. T.S. Eliot captured this best when he wrote:

> We shall not cease from exploration
> And the end of all our exploring
> Will be to arrive where we started
> And know the place for the first time.

T.S. ELIOT (1888–1965), *FOUR QUARTETS*, 'LITTLE GIDDING'

Good luck on your journey and don't be afraid of hills.

Jani Van der Veen

The Rt. Hon. The Lord Weatherill

The Retired (1992) Mr Speaker in the House of Commons

Under the title 'recreation' in *Who's Who*, I have given 'playing with my grandchildren', and that is true.

On a more serious note, I do seek to have a quiet period every evening before I go to sleep, and every morning before I get up. The former to lay aside the problems of the day, and the latter to pick them up again, very frequently with a solution! They often become very much clearer in the morning, than when I went to sleep!

Some may call this 'meditation' – and if it is I do not deny it!

Simon Weston, OBE

Falklands War Hero and Writer

I relax and unwind very much when watching rugby, having been a player once myself. I love driving and playing with James, my nine month-old baby, and sometimes having a beer with friends. I am part of quite a large family so there are many birthdays and anniversaries when I enjoy a get-together with all the family. Most of all I enjoy quiet evenings when my son is in bed and my lovely wife Lucy and I can relax together either reading or watching television.

My general philosophy of life is to live every minute to the full. Having been so near death, I love every sunrise and sunset, every day is wonderful and should be used to help, if one can, to ease others' paths. This may sound 'corny' but it was because of others helping me that I am here today.

Lastly, the quotation that has stuck in my mind since being injured is from Shakespeare's *As You Like It*:

Sweet are the uses of adversity,
Which like the toad, ugly and venomous,
Wears yet a precious jewel in his head.
WILLIAM SHAKESPEARE (1564–1616), *AS YOU LIKE IT,* ACT II, SCENE i

The toad has lovely eyes, so when people look at me, my face disfigured, I hope they look beyond that, to the person inside.

Fatima Whitbread, MBE

Former World Record Holder of the Javelin; President, Chafford Hundred Athletic Club

Each morning I leave my cottage just before 7.00 a.m., and drive to open grassland with my dog Champ. I run leisurely for about fifteen minutes, then I spend around twenty minutes in the fitness room of the local sports centre, where I partake in some general fitness exercises. Although injury forced me to retire from the competitive athletics arena, I still feel the need to maintain a high level of physical fitness and my early morning activity sets me up for the day.

After an eight-hour period in the office of Chafford Hundred Athletic Club (where I am responsible for the Club's business activities), I find that cooking an evening meal relaxes me and helps me to unwind after a stressful day.

My general philosophy of life is that one gets out of life what one puts into it and, if one is disappointed with the result, it is because God decides when one is to become an achiever.

The quotation that has provided me with determination throughout my career is 'Success comes to those who wait.' It took me twelve years to win a major athletics title – the 1986 European Championships – and with that success came the *world record*.

Mary Whitehouse, CBE

Hon. Gen. Secretary, National Viewers' and Listeners' Association 1965–80;
President since 1980; Freelance Journalist; Author

I relax and unwind whenever I possibly can by gardening – especially getting my hands in the soil!

My philosophy of life is to live in the present on the basis that I can do little about what's past and to have faith for the future.

A quotation that has inspired me:

For He walks with me, and He talks with me and He tells me that I am His own.

Mary Whitehouse

The Rt. Hon. The Lord Wilson of Rievaulx, KG, OBE, FRS

The Former British Prime Minister and Leader of the Labour Party from 1963–76

and

Lady Wilson of Rievaulx

My wife and I both relax best when we visit our small home in the Isles of Scilly where the peace and tranquillity are perfect. During the years of Government it was always a restful haven.

I am enclosing a poem from my wife, for which you asked, and would add that I have always found Rudyard Kipling's 'If' an inspiring and comforting poem.

> Primroses, daffodils, jasmine and crocus,
> Pale chilly flowers of hesitant Spring,
> Gathered with catkins and new-budded branches;
> Set in a bowl by the window, they bring
> Promise of poppies and daisies and roses –
> All the bright tangle of full summer bloom;
> Scented like lilies, austere in their beauty,
> Lighting with yellow my winter-dark room.

MARY WILSON, 'THE FLOWERS OF SPRING'

Wilson of Rievaulx.

Michael Winner

Film Director/Producer; Chairman Scimitar Films Ltd., Michael Winner Ltd., Motion Picture and Theatrical Investments Ltd. since 1957

There is nothing more relaxing than watching an open, real fire or just pottering around the garden. But as you potter around the garden picking up something here, intending to change something there, trimming a bit now and then, there enters the troubled feeling that all this is tarnished by the waste of mankind. What was once accepted as natural and pure is now beset by acid rain, pollution, the effluents of man. So relaxation becomes more difficult as we realize that the things of beauty that should give us refreshment have become a cause for concern. I also find dusting relaxing! The hoary old saying that if you've got your health you have everything is particularly true. So many of the things we complain about are insignificant when you consider the suffering of others around you in this world. I am attracted to the limerick of the 19th-century writer Adam Lindsay Gordon:

Life is mostly froth and bubble,
Two things stand like stone,
Kindness in another's trouble,
Courage in your own.

ADAM LINDSAY GORDON (1833–70), *YE WEARIE WAYFARER*, 'FYTTE 8'

Fay Woolf

Television Director and Writer

Some years ago, at a difficult time in my life, I was inspired to write an article about how I felt. I blurted it out onto a typewriter and then put it away in my desk. Thinking now about the essence of my beliefs, I realize that it stems from this crisis. Self-knowledge, if I have it, came the day I sought help, not from without, but from within . . . .

The article detailed the depths of my despair. I was unable to sleep or eat, I felt nauseous when I smelt food, I'd been vomiting and I'd lost my sense of co-ordination. An unsympathetic GP who didn't even listen to let alone hear my problems and who rabbited on instead about my gynaecological condition, referred me to an equally unhelpful specialist; I spent a fortune consulting a psychotherapist, who caused me even more angst, mainly because he wouldn't speak to me at all; in desperation I ran off to a Buddhist temple and bared my soul to a sweet monk from Thailand who told me that my mind and my body were the same and that suffering changes people (I knew that already).

And yet I *did* come through all this to a greater understanding of myself, as the end of the article reveals:

Now there wasn't anyone else to turn to but I was still thin and tired. Instead of lying awake worrying about not sleeping, I lay awake worrying about depression, stress and hypertension; latent diabetes; the tendency to anorexia in women over thirty; eye-strain; heart-strain; my sex life and my tubes. Not to mention my personality disorders and the fact that suffering changes people.

The day I felt better was the day I changed my GP, sacked the shrink and put down the Bhagavad Gita.

Fellow-sufferers, take heart and take a tip. Use the 'experts' as a last, not a first, resort. You know yourselves much better than they do. It may take time to know that you do but, when enlightenment comes, it's the ordinary things in life that are special.

Now I stick to family and friends and if any doctor, shrink or mystic is interested, I'm doing nicely thank you.

Re-reading the article six years on, I'm embarrassed by my arrogance but realize that I should perhaps be grateful for it because it helped me find the strength to survive. Instead of fighting the crisis, I gave in to it and simply chose to have a bad experience – and to take responsibility for it. Somehow, by staring darkness in the face, I regained control of my life and began to believe that this period of suffering would end. As if to reflect this optimism, a friend sent me a card with some words of Julian of Norwich on the front:

'All shall be well and all shall be well and all manner of thing shall be well.'

When I'm under pressure or feeling low and when even playing the piano or being with my children isn't helping, I go into the garden and say these words, like a mantra.

By recalling the dark, I remind myself that light did and does return. Just as gardens yield to the rhythm of Nature, by accepting that everything has its season and that seasons change, that nothing and no-one is perfect, I know I can go on, even through darkness, to the very end.

Kay Woolf

The Marchioness of Worcester

For relaxation I go for a run in the countryside.

Questions 2 and 3 – my philosophy of life and words which have inspired me – have been answered by a letter written by Chief Seattle to the US Government in 1852.

These pleas to the US Government are being repeated day after day to deaf ears as Southern Governments force indigenous people to integrate into mainstream society and the cash economy. Northern countries' development programmes are contributing to their expropriation.

We should be listening to the Indian's words if we are to reverse the present trend of environmental and social degradation:

Will you teach your children what we taught our children? That the earth is their mother? What befalls the earth befalls all the sons of the earth.

This we know: the earth does not belong to man, man belongs to the earth. All things are connected like the blood that unites us all. Man did not weave the web of life, he is merely a strand in it. Whatever he does to the web he does to himself.

One thing we know: our god is also your god. The earth is precious to him and to harm the earth is to heap contempt on its creator.

Your destiny is a mystery to us. What will happen when the buffalo are all slaughtered? The wild horses tamed? What will happen when the corners of the forest are heavy with the scent of many men and the view of the ripe hills is blotted by talking wires? Where will the thicket be? Gone! Where will the eagle be? Gone! And what is it to say goodbye to the pony and the hunt? The end of living and the beginning of survival.

When the last Red Man has vanished and his wilderness and his memory is only the shadow of a cloud moving across the prairie, will these shores and forests still be here? Will there be any of the spirit of my people left?

We love this earth as a newborn loves its mother's heartbeat. So, if we sell you our land, love it as we have loved it. Care for it as we have cared for it. Hold in your mind the memory of the land as it is when you receive it. Preserve the land for all children and love it, as God loves us all.

As we are part of the land, you too are part of the land. This earth is precious to us. It is also precious to you. One thing we know: there is only one God. No man, be he Red Man or White Man, can be apart. We are brothers after all.

Tracy Worcester

Susannah York

British Actress

I relax and unwind by getting out into Nature – gardening, walking, horse-riding. Nature is the great medicine for tension, grief . . . .

My general philosophy: 'Do as you would be done by.'

A quotation which inspires me is Thoreau's words about 'a distant drummer'. He writes that there are those who march to a different beat to that of the mob, i.e. who listen and question and follow their own instincts. It is as follows:

> If a man does not keep pace with his companions, perhaps it is because he hears a different drummer. Let him step to the music which he hears, however measured or far away.

H.D. THOREAU (1817–62), THE ILLUSTRATED WALDEN

Sir Gideon A. P. Zoleveke, KBE, MBE

Retired as Politician in the Solomon Islands in 1980; Farmer and Writer

I derive great pleasure and relaxation from writing: I have written a book, a biography of my upbringing from childhood to manhood. In the course of writing I encountered many difficulties, but these obstacles in no way interfered with my determination to complete the work. I felt great satisfaction and relief when my biography was published in book form.

My general philosophy of life has been to do things for myself and to avoid asking others to do things for me.

In my writing I have found it interesting to discover, or recover, some of the original accounts of our ancestors' and forefathers' beliefs, their activities and their way of worship. I have begun to wonder why I remember so clearly some of the poems and sayings written by others; the following quotation has never gone out of my mind:

> I expect to pass through this world but once; any good thing therefore that I can do, or any kindness that I can show to any fellow-creature, let me do it now; let me not defer or neglect it, for I shall not pass this way again.

STEPHEN GRELLET (1773–1855), FRENCH MISSIONARY

Gideon P Zoleveke

The Author

Audrey Burns Ross was born in St Andrews, Scotland. She is a registered teacher with the Scottish Yoga Teachers' Association and the British Wheel of Yoga and has taught her interpretation of yoga with emphasis on relaxation since 1968. Much of her yoga study was done with her dear friend the late Wilfred Clark, founder of the British Wheel of Yoga. She lives in central London with her husband and daughter.

The following represent some of the wise words and poems which have given me much inspiration and food for thought over the years.

Look well to this day
for it is life,
the very best of life.
In its brief course lie all
the realities and truths of existence,
  the joy of growth
  the splendour of action,
  the glory of power,
For yesterday is but a memory
and tomorrow is only a vision,
but today if well-lived makes
every yesterday a memory of happiness
and every tomorrow a vision of hope.
Look well therefore to this day.

ANCIENT SANSCRIT POEM

Do not follow where the path may lead. Go instead where there is no path and leave a trail.

SOURCE UNKNOWN

> In the calm of the autumn night
> I sit by the open window
> For whole hours in perfect
> Delightful quietness.
> The light rain of leaves falls.
> The sigh of the corruptible world
> Echoes in my corruptible nature.
> But it is a sweet sigh, it soars as a prayer.
> My window opens up a world
> Unknown. A source of ineffable,
> Perfumed memories is offered me;
> Wings beat at my window –
> Refreshing autumnal spirits
> Come unto me and encircle me
> And they speak with me in their innocent tongue.
> I feel indistinct, far-reaching hopes
> And in the venerable silence
> Of creation, my ears hear melodies,
> They hear crystalline, mystical
> Music from the chorus of the stars.

C. P. CAVAFY, 'BY THE OPEN WINDOW', FROM THE COMPLETE POEMS OF C. P. CAVAFY, TRANSLATED BY RAE DALVEN

With trust in God, with good will, self-confidence, and a hopeful attitude towards life man will always win his battle, however difficult.

HAZRAT INAYAT KHAN

Permission Acknowledgments